Fiona Fullerton loves property. Known t
theatre actress, Fiona is also a writer an
guru. For several years she wrote a popular weekly property
column in the *Saturday Telegraph* which inspired tens of
thousands to follow her advice. She now writes on property for
the *Mail on Sunday* and various other publications. Fiona runs
her own successful property business, buying, renovating and
letting flats in London and Oxford.

Recognised for her part in the Bond movie *A View to a Kill*,
Fiona has enjoyed a high-profile media presence for over 20
years. She lives in Gloucestershire with her husband Neil
Shackell, two children, two dogs and two cats.

FIONA FULLERTON'S

GUIDE TO

BUYING
TO LET

Also by Fiona Fullerton

How to Make Money From Your Property

*Fiona Fullerton's Guide to Buying,
Selling & Moving House*

FIONA FULLERTON'S

GUIDE TO

BUYING
TO LET

How to invest in the rental
market and successfully let
your property

PIATKUS

First published in 2004 by
Piatkus Books Ltd
5 Windmill Street
London W1T 2JA
e-mail: info@piatkus.co.uk

visit our website at: **www.piatkus.co.uk**

The moral right of the author has been asserted

A catalogue record for this book is available from the British Library

ISBN 0 7499 2476 4

Text design by Paul Saunders
Edited by Carol Franklin

Every effort has been made to ensure that the information
contained in this book is complete and accurate at the time of
writing. However, neither the publisher nor the author is engaged
in rendering professional advice or services to the individual
reader. The ideas and suggestions contained in this book are not
intended as a substitute for conveyancing or consulting with a legal
professional or letting agent. Neither the author nor the publisher
shall be liable or responsible for any loss or damage allegedly
arising from any information or suggestion in this book.

This book has been printed on paper manufactured with respect for the
environment using wood from managed sustainable resources

Data capture by Phoenix Photosetting, Chatham, Kent
Printed and bound in Great Britain by Mackays Ltd, Chatham, Kent

For Neil

Contents

Acknowledgements

I couldn't write a book like this without a great deal of help and support from various people who have been very generous with their time.

I would like to thank the following for their patience, research and good humour:

Alice Davis, my editor at Piatkus, for being so encouraging and patient and for letting me extend my deadline to accommodate the school holidays.

Julian Gore at Edwin Coe, my brilliant solicitor, who gives me so much legal advice and helps me to simplify things.

Betina Coulter, for putting up with me and for typing everything at lightning speed, for helping with research and for her boundless energy!

My little Lucy, for understanding that Mummy has to finish her book.

James Shacknell, for helping me with the sums!

Kym Ford, my business partner, for all her hard work on Casa Libra while I was otherwise engaged.

Annabel Stokoe, ace letting agent, for all her advice.

Ann Clayton at Lloyds, for all her financial advice.

And, of course, all the estate agents, tenants, builders, decorators, plumbers, carpet layers, plasterers, electricians and removal men who have put up with me over the years and provided me with such a rich fund of stories. To all of you I am eternally grateful and would like to say a very big thank you.

Introduction

February 27th

Help! I think I'm going bonkers. Desperation is setting in because two of my Oxford flats have been empty for six weeks. My letting agent is telling me not to panic. He says I needn't drop the rent either. I say I think I should, to make them more competitive.

March 1st

One of my London tenants rang to inform me that the boiler has finally given up the ghost. He has no hot water or heating and the temperature outside has dropped to 38°F. Great. I imagine my tenant with severe frostbite having all his toes amputated. Ring Ron to replace boiler. Bang goes my profit.

March 8th

So much for my dictum that I will never rent to students or religious fanatics. Have been convinced that new tenants will be fine. They are student religious fanatics. Truly. Four foreign chaps from the Church of Higher Day Worships are moving in. Good news is, they don't drink, smoke, watch TV or womanise. Bad news is, they will probably cook the sacrificial lamb in the middle of the drawing room.

March 11th
The religious fanatics have asked me to remove the wide-screen TV and DVD player I have just installed.

You see? Sod's Law, isn't it? Couldn't let two flats, so I installed wide-screen TVs and DVDs to attract hip young professionals. That's my market – professional, thirty-somethings. They want the latest in design and technology. So I gear my flats to that market and what happens? I get four blokes who wear open-toed sandals with socks.

Flexibility is the key word when it comes to the rental market. I've been doing this for many years now and I think it is constantly changing. I have to adapt to the market and the demands of the tenant. Once the landlord had the upper hand and the tenant would be grateful. Now the tenant is demanding and the landlord should be grateful.

Gone are the days of scummy little bedsits. The rental market is about providing a quality home for a diverse database, ranging from students to divorcees, after their million-pound divorces.

Basically, there are more people renting than ever before. The average age of the first-time buyer is now 32, so there is huge demand for rentable properties across the UK. The lettings industry is set to rise by 13 per cent over the next five years and this is probably due to employee mobility, more people in higher education, divorce rates, possible increases in interest rates, shortage of affordable housing and the availability of personal finance for investment in Buy to Let.

The Buy to Let scheme has revolutionised the rental market. In the old days, lenders would penalise the borrower if the property was a second home or was to be let, with the result that only very expensive apartments for company directors or cheap bedsits were available. There was little in between.

Now, however, the middle market has been opened up, with professional investors, like me, being able to secure special, low-cost mortgages in order to become the new breed of landlord. Some of us buy property instead of taking out a pension, whereas others are looking to boost their monthly income, but it's worth bearing in mind that the main profit lies in the capital growth of your property rather than the income received in rent.

Buying to Let isn't going to make you rich overnight. Very few people realise how complex investing in property can be and it is easy to get it wrong. I have, but I have learnt from my mistakes and this book is based on those experiences to help you avoid doing the same. The wrong property in the wrong place at the wrong price could spell disaster. But you're not going to do that, are you? If you remember to take good advice from letting agents about the type of property you should buy and who your tenant is likely to be, you won't go far wrong. They have no hidden agenda, unlike the estate agent who is trying to sell to you.

There is a new type of tenant now with a higher disposable income and a stylish lifestyle that needs to be reflected in their home environment, and the good thing about Buy to Let is that it has shaken out the dodgy landlords with the old-style properties and brought in the younger investor. To succeed as a landlord, your property has to have a fashionable edge and flexibility is most important. You have to be prepared to live with the fluctuations in the rental market, the void periods, the highs and lows. If you have money to invest in a second property and are prepared to take the heat, then go for it.

For reasons of simplicity I always refer to the landlord in the male gender and to the tenant as he, him and his. I do hope nobody takes offence. Also, when researching this book I have tried to be as accurate as possible, however, legislation changes frequently, as do the interest rates. This book is not meant to be a professional guide to conveyancing or a substitute for the need to take legal advice, it is merely to guide you through the process of investing in the private rental sector.

Fiona Fullerton 2004

CHAPTER 1

Should you be investing in Buy to Let?

Am I the sort of person who should be a landlord?

As a landlord what *could* I be letting?

Understanding the private rental sector

Am I the sort of person who should be a landlord?

If you're mad enough, yes! You need to be fairly brave and prepared to get your hands dirty. People are always amazed when I tell them that I've just been cleaning the showerhead/painting the front door/taking down curtains, etc. in one of my flats. But who else is going to do it when we are fledgling landlords? It may be different when you have built up your portfolio and can afford to hire in people, but until then, these are the questions you need to ask yourself:

- Are you prepared to do some fairly physical tasks, such as moving furniture and redecorating? You do need to be fit.

- Do you understand the financial risks?

- Do you have enough spare time? (I'm assuming you have regular employment.)

- Are you willing to take advice?

- Can you communicate easily with people?

- Are you organised?

- Are you prepared to accept responsibility regarding safety regulations?

Being a landlord is definitely quite stressful at times, but once you have decided to invest in the private rental sector there are various ways to ensure that you get it right, make a profit and even have fun. If you wanted an easy life you'd just stick your capital in the building society and watch it grow. But that's boring. That's no fun at all. You obviously want to do something more exciting with your money and, like me, you quite enjoy a challenge.

As it stands at the moment, I pay 10 per cent to my letting agent to find a good, paying tenant, check the references, draw up the contract and everything else is down to me. I could always pass the management of the property on to my agent and let them deal with the problems, but I would pay an extra 5 per cent of the rental for that luxury and every hiccup afterwards would cost me an arm and a leg, so I don't. (See Chapter 6, Letting Your Property Through an Agent.)

The secret to staying sane as a landlord is to have a good back-up team and an organised filing system. It helps if you have a tame plumber or carpenter whom you can call out in an emergency and someone strong to help with humping all the furniture around. The filing system is necessary because you need to keep tabs on when your gas safety certificate is up for renewal or your inventory needs updating.

I love being a landlord, but have to confess that there have been times when the frustrations of dealing with an awkward tenant and trying to find my plumber when the washing machine has just exploded, have been so immense that I just wanted to chuck it all in. But I am glad I didn't. If you possess tenacity, determination and strength you will become a successful landlord.

As a landlord what *could* I be letting?

There are many different ways of making money out of letting and they don't all have to be Bought to Let. For instance, I heard about a lady in Shoeburyness who ran a little bed and breakfast for 14 years before renting out a room to a visiting businessman on an annual basis. She now has 32 rental properties, borrowing on each of them as they increase in value! Well, it can happen.

Renting out a room

You could start by renting out a room in your own home. Supposing the children have flown the nest (or the husband has) and your place suddenly feels very large. You could make your home pay for itself and have a nice bit of unearned income by renting out a room or two. This is simple to achieve by local advertising or word of mouth. Place an ad with a nearby company whose employees are looking for accommodation.

Ask around for advice on what to charge and set clear guidelines with your tenant about the use of the kitchen and bathroom etc. If you can provide a separate bathroom, so much the better. Set rules about socialising and entertaining, otherwise you could find yourself swamped by a steady stream of visitors. Check the potential tenant's credentials and employment status, and you could even ask to see their last bank statement. Always get a month's rent up front.

If you rent out a room you are liable to pay tax after an allowance of £4,250 per annum, which is tax free.

CHECKLIST

Advertise locally. ☐

Ask advice on what to charge. ☐

Set clear guidelines on use of kitchen and bathroom. ☐

Set rules on socialising hours and entertaining. ☐

Don't let them pass the key on to their friends. ☐

Check their credentials. ☐

Get a reference and ask for last bank statement. ☐

Get a month's rent up front. ☐

Multi-occupancy

Of course, if you have the space you could rent out more than one room, but as soon as you get into the realms of multi-occupancy, there are specific regulations that you would need to observe regarding extra fire safety and the maintenance of the communal parts. Your local authority will advise you on this.

CHECKLIST

Speak to your local authority. ☐

Be aware of specific regulations. ☐

See above checklist for renting out a room. ☐

Self-contained accommodation

If you have self-contained accommodation, such as a granny annexe or a basement flat that has its own kitchen and bathroom, it could be ideal for letting. Ask a local letting agent for advice on rentals and what to charge. The agent will recommend you draw up an Assured Shorthold Tenancy Agreement with your tenant to avoid any problems (see page 104) and of course will be angling for the job of letting it for you. If you decide to go it alone the same rules apply as if it were a Buy to Let rental property, i.e. if you want to achieve the same rent as the rest of the market you will need to identify your target market and present the flat accordingly (see page 36). You will also need to abide by the various regulations concerning gas, fire and electricity.

CHECKLIST

Ask a local letting agent for advice. ☐

Make sure your property matches the right tenant
(i.e. student or young couple). ☐

Get an inventory drawn up if it is furnished. ☐

Be aware of landlord's obligations. ☐

Regard regulations. ☐

Draw up a proper agreement. ☐

Renting out your home

Alternatively, you could rent out your entire home if your circumstances allow it, for example, if you are relocating to another
part of the country or getting married. Often, newlyweds fall into
the rental market by circumstance. Two young people, each with
their own flat, get married and have one flat surplus to requirements. So it is let and they can appreciate the capital growth until
they really need to sell it. All the above rules apply, but I would say,
having done it myself, that renting out your own home – your
very personal space – is very different from entering the Buy to
Let market. It is an emotional personal decision, whereas letting a
rental property is a business decision and has no emotion
attached to it. If you intend to return to your home in the future,
after it has been let, I would strongly recommend that you use a
good letting agent who will thoroughly vet the candidates and
that you pay for the management of the property, so that if something breaks down you do not have to deal with it. The agent will.
There is nothing more soul-destroying than walking into your
home when other people have moved in and thrown all their
'stuff' around the place. It feels like an invasion.

Just think about the income and the capital growth and don't visit the place until after they have moved out and it has been cleaned.

CHECKLIST

Use a reputable letting agent who is a member of ARLA (Association of Residential Letting Agents – see Useful Addresses). ☐

Negotiate for them to do the management. ☐

Remove any precious possessions. ☐

Get an inventory. ☐

Tell your mortgage lender. ☐

Be aware that it could be emotional for you. ☐

CASE STUDY

Some friends of mine live in Wimbledon and move out for two weeks every summer. Why? Because they can make an absolute fortune during the tennis championships letting their four-bedroomed (fairly average) house to some tennis player with an unpronounceable name, his family and his coach. If you live near a similar hot spot this could be worth bearing in mind.

Of course, there are other circumstances, such as letting a property that you have inherited, but these are the main ways of entering the rental market without buying a property to do so. This is exactly how I became involved in letting. I was living in Central London and needed to go to the United States for 18 months, so I let my flat to a very nice couple from Chile. This gave me the bug for being a landlord!

If you can do none of the above and are starting out in the rental market by buying a second property specifically as an investment, or have already started expanding your portfolio, then this is the book for you. So read on.

Understanding the private rental sector

Unfortunately, there is no magic formula to guarantee that you will always get it right. Letting tends to follow trends in the local property sales market. When the housing market is depressed and property is 'sticking', it is often difficult to let as well. When the market is buoyant and property is moving, it is easier to let.

This doesn't make it any easier for us landlords but it does mean that your property must be chosen wisely. Follow the local lettings market for a while and visit some currently available flats, to see what the competition might be offering. It is imperative that you have researched the area and asked the local agents whether there is demand for rental properties and that it is not likely to dry up.

Have you decided to use an agent or are you going it alone? (See page 92.) What sort of tenant do you want to attract? These are just some of the questions that are a part of the pre-planning. In the old days I would just buy a flat that appealed to me, do it up and then instruct a letting agent to let it. I cringe now at my naivety because it could never be that simplistic. If this is going to be your major investment, you need to assess its market potential. The following checklist will help you to minimise the risks:

CHECKLIST

Have you found out about the current market? ☐

Is there demand in the area? ☐

Choose the property, and location, with care. ☐

Make sure the lease has more than 60 years to run, in case you want to sell on. ☐

Have you identified your market? ☐

Will you be using a local agent or not? ☐

Be prepared for void periods. ☐

Have you budgeted for furniture? ☐

Are you prepared to lower the rent if you need to? ☐

The bottom line is, in order to understand the private rental sector (that is, providing a home for people who need somewhere to live as opposed to people who need somewhere to trade or to work), you need to approach it as a business venture with possible financial risks. Ideally it will be profitable – you have the capital profit, or capital growth, which is in the increase of the market value of your property, and you have the income profit (there is more on this on page 18). But there will be times (or may be times) when the property is empty and the demand has fallen away.

Dangers and warnings

An empty rental property is definitely not a desirable situation. Known as a 'void' period (or sometimes as 'down time'), this is when your property is not producing an income and therefore is costing you money. It is inevitable that there will be some void periods, such as:

- the time it takes between buying the property and doing any renovations prior to letting

- the turnaround time between tenancies (this is when I redecorate or replace items and freshen it up)

- the state of the market and the strength of your property within that market (How does it shape up against the competition?).

The main danger is when the whole climate changes after a disaster such as 9/11 or during a time of political unrest. This will affect, obviously, many different elements, including the rental market. Fewer tenants means hungry landlords. Foreign tenants seem to evaporate at these times, so in 2001 I was forced to lower my rents in order to make my properties affordable for the home market. (For more on what to do to attract tenants, see page 154.)

QUESTIONS YOU SHOULD ASK YOURSELF BEFORE BUYING TO LET

Q Is there plenty of demand in this area?

Q Will this property let easily? (See Identifying Your Target Market page 36.)

Q What will my capital growth be?

Q How much should I spend on doing it up?

Q What are the overall running costs? Can I afford the void periods?

Q What is the likely annual rental?

Q Set against the purchase price, what is my yield? Am I over-
looking any hidden costs?

Hopefully, questions like these will prepare you for your new life
as a landlord. But don't forget the tax inspector. He just loves
unearned income. However, you can set your mortgage interest
repayments off against your rental income and only pay tax on
the profit after costs. But, remember, if you are borrowing money,
the main profit lies in the capital growth. Never borrow too much,
otherwise the voids really eat into your profit.

CHAPTER 2

Understanding the finances

Doing the sums

Organising your finance

Raising the money to buy

Understanding taxation

What will I need to pay for?

Doing the sums

Remember that buying a rental property is very different from buying your own home and it is easy to let emotion intervene. Big mistake, believe me. The financial aspect of Buying to Let is the most crucial element. The capital profit of your property must be taken into account in looking at your investment as a whole. Once you have found the property you want to buy, you can raise a loan against it – a special Buy to Let mortgage at normal rates, which is available through most banks and building societies – and the rent you receive should cover the monthly repayments and other expenses, leaving you, hopefully, with a profit. If you are a cash buyer with no loans, then you are into pure profit.

What is a yield?

Yield is another word for the profit you make on your rental income. It is normally quoted as the gross profit. (I would be very happy indeed with 10 per cent but would happily settle for 5 or 6 per cent.) You then need to make all the deductions of your costs, such as the loan, taxation, expenses, etc. (see page 27) and you will be left with your net profit – or net yield. Some landlords do not make much annual profit because as long as it 'washes its face', in other words pays for itself and covers costs, they are only interested in the capital growth.

However, if you are dependent on the net profit then it becomes a slightly more risky situation because you can never tell when a horrid void period is going to come along. This is when a cheap flat, attaining high rent, will offer the highest yield. The lower end of the market will usually produce the greatest yields. For example, if you bought a flat for £140,000 and were making £14,000 rental income, then your yield would be 10 per cent. On the other hand, if you rented a large family house that cost

£450,000 for £36,000 per annum, your yield would be only 8 per cent. The most obvious way to make a bigger annual profit is to buy a flat that is in terrible condition, do it up yourself and then let it to a higher end sort of tenant. This is what I usually do. The turnaround has to be quick though because every week it is empty is a 'void' week where you have no paying tenant. I try to have my flats ready for rental within four weeks. The void periods in any lettings play havoc with your sums, so I always base my projected rental income on 46 weeks of the year, which allows for six void weeks for turnaround between tenants. Some years, of course, this may not happen if you have a tenant on a long let.

Organising your finance

If you are thoroughly convinced that you understand what it takes to be a landlord, you will have to start looking at your own finances and decide how much you can afford to put down as a capital deposit before you approach a lender for the balance.

Write down what savings or funds you may have. Most lenders will only lend around 75 per cent of the value of the property, so it is up to you to find the remaining 25 per cent. By now you will probably already have started looking around at what property is available, so you will have some idea of the sums involved.

For example: you may have saved £3,000, which is in a building society account, your aunt has left you £4,000, which is still in another account, you are borrowing £20,000 against your own home, which has increased in value, and have a small bonus coming into your current account at the end of the month.

Ideally, you need to gather all these funds together and place them in a high interest account. As it is quite a substantial amount, check around for the best possible rate.

Ask for advice

You could always ask for professional advice to make sure you are doing the right thing. It could be from:

- a solicitor

- your bank manager

- a letting agent

- an accountant

- an independent financial adviser.

These are all people who can assist in the decision-making process and help you to understand the financial liabilities.

Raising the money to buy

CASE STUDIES

Q. Carole has inherited a flat from her granny. Should she let it after refurbishment, borrow against it to buy another flat or sell it?

A. Assuming there are no outstanding loans on the property, she could borrow money against it to buy another property (this means that a lender would let her borrow money based on the value of the property in order for her to reinvest), and take on a small mortgage on both properties; she is then the landlord of **two** properties.

Q. Roger would like to Buy to Let. He has a mortgage on his own home of £100,000, the property now being worth £140,000. He has £5,000 saved in capital, so could he borrow £60,000 to buy a small flat for rental?

A. The sums don't really add up. If he intends to put down only £5,000 deposit, he would be unlikely to secure a loan of £60,000. However, if he waits a while for his home to increase in value, he would then be able to borrow more as a deposit.

Many people think that you need to be fairly wealthy to invest in Buy to Let, but that is not true. There are lots of ways to get started but hard work and the ability to save are obviously dominant factors. (And slightly obvious.)

I know of investors who worked long hours doing two jobs, in order to save enough capital to buy their second property. (The first being their home.) Having the vision and the dedication has led to a very comfortable lifestyle with houses in the South of France and a Ferrari in the garage! So, it can be done.

Here are the various ways you can get started.

Use your savings

This is the money you have squirrelled away in your bank account or building society to put down as a deposit on your first rental property. You should have it on a high interest account, although there will be some lost interest when you take the money out, until the property is rented.

Use your home to raise a mortgage

Assuming you own the home you currently live in, you can remortgage the whole property to release some equity to pay for the deposit. Your home is increasing in value all the time, so most lenders are happy to do this. Or, you can keep the existing mortgage the same and borrow on the remaining equity.

> For example: you own a flat worth £100,000 and have £30,000 left to pay on the mortgage. The lender will only give you 85 per cent of the value of your property, which is £85,000 so: £85,000 minus £30,000 = £55,000.

So you now have £55,000 to invest. You buy a flat for £50,000 and, after doing all your sums, you are sure you can get a rent of £400 per month.

In order to raise the loan you will need to prove to the bank or building society that your income will cover the repayments. Bear in mind the following points:

- Your loan should not be more than 3 times your income or 2.5 times if you are buying with a partner.

- The loan should not be more than the specified percentage of the value of the property (i.e. 85 per cent).

- An experienced mortgage broker could give you excellent advice on what will suit your needs. Shop around.

- The rental income may be considered by some lenders.

Sell some assets

You may have a painting that your granny left you or a collection of toy trains that could go to an auction. Real cash can be made from selling off assets such as these. Have a think. Maybe you could offer to split the proceeds if your mother wishes to make you a gift of the contents of that trunk in the attic. Auction houses will give you realistic valuations.

Sell your shares

Seek professional advice from a financial adviser or stockbroker if you think now is a good time to sell your shares or to surrender an endowment policy. You may be wise to put that money into property instead.

Borrow money from a family member

You could either borrow some money and offer to pay it back later with interest, or you could ask for access to any money you feel you may inherit (a bit cheeky but many people do this) in order to avoid inheritance tax. As long as the person who gives you the money – usually a parent – lives for another seven years, there will be no inheritance tax payable, which is excellent all round.

Use a Buy to Let mortgage

Ah, the Buy to Let mortgage. This, for me, is the most obvious route to go down, because you are raising the loan using the rental property as security. It is a blissfully straightforward way of getting a mortgage for your first rental investment, as long as you have sufficient funds to put down as a deposit.

What is a Buy to Let mortgage?

It was introduced, as luck would have it, just as I was getting involved in the rental market in 1994–5. It is a specially tailored mortgage which allows you to buy a flat or house for letting. Prior to this, mortgage companies would charge a higher rate if you wanted to become a landlord, but this is the case no more. It allows you to borrow the money based on the capital value of the property and the proposed rental income, rather than your personal income.

However, you do need a larger deposit as most lenders will only lend a maximum of 75–85 per cent of the purchase price. So, for a flat costing £100,000 you may only get £75,000 and will need to find the rest. (This is when you need to start raiding the attic.)

The reason for the higher deposit is because with a Buy to Let mortgage the property has to be successfully let to cover the payments. This presents a higher risk to the lender.

What can you afford?

The amount you can put down as a deposit will dictate how much you can borrow.

> For example:
> You have £6,000 to invest.
> The lender will only give you 85 per cent.
> Therefore, your maximum purchase price is: £40,000.

It is really important to know how much you can afford, otherwise you will be wasting time looking at properties that are not within your budget.

Take advice on Buy to Let mortgages because there are a lot around and there is bound to be one that suits you. Go into a bank, contact an IFA (independent financial adviser) or a mortgage broker and tell them what you want. It will depend on various things, such as:

- how much investment or savings you have

- the price of the property

- the type or style of property

- the perceived rental income

- your credit history.

> Most lenders would like the rent to be about 25–30 per cent higher than the mortgage payments to allow for void periods or a rise in interest rates. This is why research is so important. No point investing in an area that is already over-supplied.

As with a mortgage on your own home where you are the owner-occupier, you can choose from:

- capped rate mortgage – these will go up and down but never rise above the 'capped' limit

- variable – these fluctuate with the Bank of England's interest rates

- fixed rate – rate is 'fixed' regardless of what the Bank of England is up to.

Points to remember

Interest on mortgage repayments can be offset against rental income for tax purposes (see page 27), so I always go for interest-only payments, where the capital loan is not repaid until you sell the property.

Some lenders are cautious about lending money on certain types of property and they are:

- studio flats

- ex-council houses or flats

- property above a shop or restaurant

- flats above the fourth floor

- property of unusual construction.

Ask the lender what other exclusions there might be. They may, for example, not lend to you if your tenant is likely to be a DSS claimant or a student.

Understanding taxation

So here comes the boring bit. Talking about tax makes me do one of two things. Either yawn or get very, very cross. Unfortunately it is a very necessary part of the whole Buy to Let structure and must be fully understood. (A good accountant, let me say, is invaluable because he or she will advise you on the various complications that can, and will, arise.)

Of course, tax must be taken into account when doing your sums so that you can correctly predict your net profit.

There are two different types of tax which affect us landlords:

- income tax

- capital gains tax (CGT).

This is what you need to know.

Income tax

Basically, the profit on the rent you receive from your property is like income and is therefore liable to income tax.

> There are many allowances and because your rental income is only a part of your overall income, each individual situation is unique, so it is important that you seek professional advice.

In order to find out how much you owe the taxman (or woman) you need to:

- add up all the rental income for that tax year

- deduct your expenses and any other allowances

- whatever is left is now added to your other income (assuming you have some other employment) to assess your tax liability at whatever the current rate may be, e.g. rental income minus expenses = taxable amount.

> If you have made a loss, this can usually be carried forward to future tax years and used to offset a profit. (Deduct it from your future profit.)

Allowable expenses

There are lots of lovely things you can claim against tax as a landlord. (However, I do recommend that you check with your local tax office first.) They are:

- letting agents' fees

- rates or council tax

- insurance premiums

- bills for utilities

- lease renewal expenses

- interest and charges on your finance

- travel to and from the property

- 10 per cent wear and tear

- legal fees in seeking advice

- replacing or upgrading furniture.

Wear 'n' tear

If you let the property furnished, you can claim 10 per cent of your net rental income to cover the repairs or replacements of items that have been subjected to wear and tear. However, if you choose to claim the 10 per cent, you cannot also claim for specific items, which would normally be covered by the allowance.

So, for example, if I am doing a major refurbishment in one of the flats that requires a new bathroom, redecoration throughout and some new furniture, I will claim for all that because it could amount to more than 10 per cent, but waive my 10 per cent wear 'n' tear. You can't have both.

More often than not, depending on your individual circumstances, it may be better to claim each expense separately under 'renewals' and provide the receipts.

> You do not pay income tax separately from your other income – it is always combined. If you don't have any other income, you will not pay tax unless your rental profit is greater than your personal tax allowances.

Capital gains tax

Capital gains tax (CGT) is extremely complicated territory and is the one subject that I receive the most letters and emails about. It seems everyone is mystified by capital gains tax but here is a very simple guide.

Please remember, I am not a qualified accountant (in fact, even a qualified accountant will groan when I ask about CGT), so it is important you take your unique capital gains tax enquiries to a professional.

There are many sources available to you who could provide helpful information:

- your accountant

- your bank manager

- local tax office

- special tax advisory firm

- printed matter from the Inland Revenue or special magazines and books

- the internet.

What is capital gains tax?

It is a tax you pay on any profit you make on the sale of your property. This only applies to a property that is *not* your home or principal private residence (PPR). It is based on the difference between the buying and selling price, minus various allowances.

For example: you buy a rental property purely as an investment for £80,000. You spend £10,000 doing it up and sell it four years later for £120,000. Your liability will be based on the £30,000, which is the *increase* in the value of the property after certain allowances.

The *expenses* and *allowances* you can set against CGT are many and varied, but in summary consist of the following:

- Acquisition costs: this is the amount you actually paid to buy the property. If you inherited the property, the market value is taken on the day of the transfer into your name.

- Enhancement costs: this is the expense of upgrading or modernising the property and getting it ready for resale. Everything from converting the basement to adding double-glazing are considered to be 'enhancements'. However, if you have got rid of an enhancement – built a garage then knocked it down – you would not be able to include those costs.

- Incidental costs: these are the costs of actually buying and selling the property. They include:

  - legal fees for your solicitor and surveyor
  - conveyancing costs
  - estate agents' commission
  - stamp duty
  - advertising costs.

- Other legal costs: you can deduct other things such as any disputes you may have had over the property that incurred legal fees etc.

Here are some additional points to remember:

- We all have an annual CGT personal allowance and only pay CGT if our profit exceeds this figure. This amount changes from time to time.

- If you haven't made a profit there will be no CGT to pay.

- You only pay CGT when you sell a property that is *not* your 'primary residence' (home).

- Any profit or loss must be added to any other properties you may be selling in order to assess your CGT. (If one makes a loss and the other makes a profit, they *could* cancel each other out. Ask your accountant.)

- If you bought the rental property before March 1982 you can choose to use the market value as of March 1982. This is very good news if you bought it in 1957! (Because it will lessen your taxable profit.)

- You only pay CGT on the *increase* in value of your property.

> If your rental property was *once your home*, but you now live elsewhere, you may get even more relief on your CGT bill. Yippee! But it does depend on how long you let your property, how much of it you let if you still lived there and whether the letting took place within the last three years.

Taper relief

This is another way of reducing your CGT liability, which was introduced in April 1998. The simple principle is that the longer you have owned the property, the less tax you pay. A calculation will be made by your tax office or tax adviser.

Questions to ask a tax adviser

It is always advisable to use someone who has been personally recommended to you. An accountant or adviser will need to know your whole financial situation so you will need to provide full details.

Q Can you advise me on income tax *and* capital gains tax?

Q Are you experienced with the rules relating to rental income?

Q Would you complete my tax return form for me?

Q What services do you offer?

Q How do you charge?

Q How long will it take?

Q What records do I need to keep?

Q Where can I get other information?

There are no loopholes. Only good advice.

Capital gains tax in Scotland

The rules and exemptions are much the same as in England and Wales, where if you own two homes and spend some time living in each of them, for example a flat in town during the week and a cottage in the country at weekends, the exemption will only extend to one of the two. Broadly you have the choice as to which one benefits from the exemption, but it is important to 'pre-select' your choice by notifying the Inland Revenue within certain time limits. Similarly, if you have a rental property you will only be exempt from CGT on your primary residence.

What will I need to pay for?

There are many expenses and hidden costs to take into account when doing your sums, for example:

mortgage repayments
agency fees
other professional fees
service charges (if any)
stamp duty
Land Registry fees
council tax when the property
  is empty
insurance
advertising

Gas Safety Certificate
redecorating
inventory clerk
updating furniture
advertising
repairs and maintenance
wear and tear
taxation
utilities bills
cleaning between tenants

When the property is let the tenant is usually responsible for utility bills and council tax, but when the property is empty this becomes the landlord's responsibility. If you are furnishing the property then obviously this is an added expense, which should be budgeted into your 'setting-up costs'. Good furniture can be expensive and you cannot charge tenants for normal wear and tear. (See page 28.) This usually means that I have to replace mattresses and sofas approximately every five years.

A service charge is payable by the landlord in most leasehold properties as this covers the maintenance of the common parts and building insurance, etc. The service charge will also provide a sinking fund for any major expenditure (such as roof repairs). It will include:

- the cleaning of all the common parts, such as corridors and the reception area

- the maintenance of any lifts

- the entry-phone

- porter's salary (if any)

- pest control

- buildings insurance

- the lighting in the common parts

- general maintenance.

Agency fees can vary between 8 per cent and 20 per cent, depending on the service that the letting agent is providing. This is assuming that you are using a letting agent (which I always recommend) and not letting it yourself. Their fees will exclude VAT.

CHAPTER 3

Choosing the right property

Identifying your target market

Finding a property

Identifying your target market

Before you invest in the rental market it is crucial that you can clearly identify your target market. In other words, who is your tenant likely to be? Obviously, there is a very wide choice and the price, location, style and decor of the property will all come into play once you have decided which end of the market to target. I mean, if you buy a student let you don't want it to be in the most expensive part of town where they loathe bicycles.

Similarly, if you are going for the corporate let, those tenants will need more space for entertaining and will expect very high quality furnishings.

It is a fact that the properties that are the most up to date, recently decorated, well presented and well equipped will let the fastest. Young professionals, with their disposable income, demand apartments within high specification new developments in desirable locations. They like high-tech designer living. It is an extension of their designer-led, label-conscious lifestyle. All my rental properties are aimed at people who fall into this bracket, but you may be more interested in letting to:

- groups of students

- a single student

- group of single people

- a single person

- a couple

- a family

- an elderly couple (retirement home).

Are you interested in providing luxury accommodation or budget accommodation? You will need to assess where the demand lies in your target area. For example, you may find that family homes are in short supply and that there is a surplus of one-bedroom flats. Your budget may be insufficient to buy a three-bedroom family house, so you will have to think again.

What do I buy?

With so many single young professionals and first-time buyers leaving it until they are 32 to buy, according to statistics, the biggest demand in the market is for one-bedroom flats. Even the more affluent 30-somethings want to rent because it gives them flexibility and mobility.

I have both one-bedroom and two-bedroom flats and the one-bedders are always the easier to let. Admittedly, these are all in city locations, but research shows that it is the same up and down the UK. Further away from the cities, but still within easy commuting distance, the larger family houses are very much in demand. This is due to relocation of families visiting from abroad on two- or three-year secondments.

Every part of the UK has its rental market but obviously it differs greatly from area to area. It is always best to seek advice from a letting agent if you are thinking of investing. She (and I say she because it is nearly always ladies in lettings) will know what the requirement is for in your area. Here are some examples:

- In a university town she may suggest you buy a small terraced house and let to four students.

- She may suggest a house on a brand-new estate for an executive in one of the local corporations.

- In the heart of Surrey she may suggest a family home near the American school.

- In a city she may suggest a flat in an area that is currently undergoing regeneration.

The only areas I would stay away from are the very rural countryside and obvious tourist traps such as Stratford-upon-Avon. These are great for holiday homes but that is a very different section of the rental market. (See Chapter 10, Investing in the Holiday Rental Market.)

Having identified your target market you will need to draw up a list of your ideal accommodation to show the estate agent. Here's a checklist to take with you:

CHECKLIST

One bedroom or two? ☐

Bathroom and separate toilet? ☐

Kitchen with separate eating area? ☐

Sitting room with office area? ☐

Storage? ☐

Dining room? ☐

My one-bedroom flats tend to be fairly small but with plenty of light and a good outlook. I have one bedroom, a large sitting room, small kitchen and bathroom.

Also, you will need to state clearly the area that you are targeting and your price limit. Check for desirable extras such as off-street parking, garaging and outbuildings for storage.

Whether you buy a house or a flat very much depends on the demand. I would say start small and see how it goes. If you have inherited a property I would spend some money bringing it right up to date because tenants are getting fussier these days and, with so much choice, your property will need to have an edge. With the arrival of Buy to Let mortgages came an influx of new landlords all keen to invest in the private rental sector. This increased supply so much that the tenant was suddenly offered a remarkable choice. He wanted wood flooring. He demanded power showers and an eye-level cooker! This flushed out the older generation of landlords with a 'That'll do' philosophy and means that now, if you want to attract the upper-end professional, your property must be highly attractive. A well-presented property will always let more quickly than a run-of-the-mill one.

Studio flats – a warning!

A studio flat is definitely a risky proposition because given the choice a tenant would much rather have a separate bedroom. I know this from experience, having bought a studio flat in London, spent oodles doing it up and was then unable to let it. They may have limited appeal at the upper end of the market but at the lower end it is a different story.

'Obviously they are popular with students,' said one agent I spoke to, 'because it is usually all they can afford. But 400 sq ft can be difficult to sell. Developers are choosing not to include them in projects any more because they use up far too much land.'

A studio flat tends to have a ceiling price so it is a mistake to throw loads of money at it if the property simply isn't worth it. You must remember the potential capital growth of your property and not just its 'letability' factor. However, having said that, in the right location (i.e. close to a university) it could be just the thing for a student.

Recognising the potential of a property

This is exactly the same as when one is buying a home for oneself, because the quickest way to a bargain is to buy something that no one else wants.

You know those *House Doctor* programmes? The thing that they identify is that most buyers lack imagination and, when presented with some ghastly decor, they usually do not buy. As a result, a property can 'stick' on the market for some time. This is where you come in and snap it up!

So try to look past all the personal knick-knacks and fuchsia wallpaper to assess the potential letability of the property. It's amazing what can be achieved by ripping out dodgy carpets and throwing lots of white paint on the walls. Look out for features such as fireplaces, windows that let in lots of light and easy access.

CASE STUDY

I bought a flat in 1997, direct from the vendor, that had been a student squat for four years. It had turquoise carpets, swirly wallpaper and disgusting green bathrooms. It had three bedrooms but the living room had also been used as a bedroom. It was really, really horrible, but, and this is a big but, it was in the middle of Kensington and had its own parking space. I bought it and transformed it and let it to a major corporation for two years, making approximately 12 per cent yield.

Sadly, the market changed, so I had to drop the rent dramatically but it was still a good buy.

Where do I buy?

Location, as ever, is crucial when Buying to Let. Tenants need easy access to transport links such as rail, road and bus. Even students don't like to cycle too far to their campus and you will find that there are hot spots in the university towns where they *do* like to live.

Most tenants, corporate or otherwise, like to be fairly close to the local amenities, such as cinemas, parks and restaurants. If you are buying out of town you will need to consider whether the property has a parking space, how far the railway station is and where the nearest school is (if it's a family home).

You must research the area thoroughly before making any decisions about where to buy because the neighbourhood and environment will reflect enormously on your success in the rental market and, of course, if you were to sell. Having made several mistakes myself on identifying prime rental areas I can assure you that a tenant will be just as fussy about where he lives as an owner-occupier.

On-street parking could be a problem, for example, for a smart young city type who takes enormous pride in his wheels. However, if you are catering for the student market then obviously this isn't going to be an issue.

- One-bedroom flats are the easiest to let.

- Stay away from very rural areas.

- Avoid studio flats unless you're aiming at the student market.

- Victorian houses in university towns offer good yields to the investor.

- Buy close to road and rail links with a fast route into the nearest city.

- Buy close to local amenities such as restaurants and cinemas.

- Target a specific sort of tenant.

- Don't buy a flat in a shabby block where the hallways and stairs are in need of attention.

- Don't buy in a known 'dodgy' street.

- Security is important.

- A flat with a terrace or nice view will always let well.

- A family house with a garden, within easy commuting distance of the nearest city will command a premium.

Remember, the basic principles of buying property apply. Even though this is an investment property you must still assess its market potential and saleability for it to represent a suitable investment. In my opinion, there is little point spending on a rental investment that has little or no potential when you want to sell. Remember that your biggest profit lies in the capital growth of the property, so in an ideal world you need to buy with a view to a long-term investment. The longer you keep it, the more you make. Many a landlord has come a cropper (and I include myself in this one) by making a bum decision about a property and being forced to sell within two years. Not good. The CGT you pay makes the entire exercise almost fruitless.

The chart opposite will help you to identify your tenant and what they need.

Be adventurous

In an area with a high demand for reasonable rental accommodation, such as Oxford, why not buy a house and convert it into flats? Of course, you will need planning permission and building regulation approval first, which usually takes at least eight weeks to obtain. Check with the planning department of the local authority and find out what their attitude is to such an application – they are usually very helpful. This could make sound

The tenant	Type of let	Area	Amenities	Type of property
Students	Long let 3–4 years	University towns	Pubs, clubs, cinemas	Large house with four to five bedrooms or studio flat
Single professionals	6–12 months	Any city or large town	Smart restaurants, shops, clubs	One-bedroom flat
Young couples mid range	6–12 months	Any city or large town	Smart restaurants, shops, parks	One/two-bedroom flat
Corporate tenant – upper	6 months to 4 years	Cities or rural commutable	Schools, gyms, restaurants	Large two/three-bedroom flat or house
Family	6 months to 4 years	Commuter belt	Parks, schools, leisure centres	Four-bedroom house

investment sense for letting. Take good advice before buying anything though, because the local agent might tell you that there is nil demand for flats in her area and to stick with the house. Some areas or streets are clearly designated as 'house' streets or 'flat' streets.

Letting to housing associations

As a landlord it is possible to fill your property with tenants who are on benefit or social security or, indeed, who may have some disability. These tenants would be placed by your local council housing department and your legal commitment and liability would be with them. Letting to housing associations can be risky simply due to the type of tenant. They may be asylum seekers, refugees or unemployed, and could be fairly heavy on the wear and tear. However, this is not to say that it is not financially rewarding, but it can mean a lot more work regarding maintenance and repairs.

The term 'housing associations' is a generic term for organisations legally known as registered social landlords.

A registered social landlord (RSL) is the technical name for landlords who are registered with the Housing Corporation under the Housing Act 1996 – most are housing associations, but there are also trusts, co-operatives and companies.

Finding a property

The most important thing to remember is that you are now looking for a property that you are going to rent to someone else on a business basis, purely as an investment. This is not going to be a home for *you*. You must be subjective so, having done all your research and made your decisions regarding your ideal tenant, you need to start looking for the perfect property to fit your remit. Where do you start? Well, there are lots of different avenues to explore:

- estate agents' offices

- newspaper and private advertisements

- the internet

- the auction rooms.

Estate agents

If you go to an estate agent, take your list of requirements with you and be very specific about your needs, i.e. 'I'm looking for a one-bedroom flat, with lounge, kitchen, bathroom, on a long lease, within a five-mile radius of Leeds city centre, between £85,000 and £100,000, in need of modernisation.'

Don't be put off if the agent says he has nothing on the market like that at the moment; just leave your details and ask him to keep in touch, then start trawling around all the other agents.

Of course, you could go to an area that you have identified as ideal and look around for 'For Sale' boards, then ring the relevant agents and ask them about the property. While you are on the phone, you will need to ask them:

- the price

- the number of rooms

- the condition of the property

- the length of the lease

- its suitability.

Only agree to a viewing if it meets your criteria, otherwise you will be wasting time.

When you are viewing a property, you must remember to put your emotions and your first impressions on hold. I know this is difficult because when you walk into a property you either go 'Yuk' or 'Wow'. We all make a decision based on the first 30 seconds of what we see, but in the rental market it is important to envisage what the tenant might be thinking as he or she walks in for the first time.

When I view properties I have an imaginary tenant called Roger who is loosely based on a single professional mate of mine.

As I view a flat (one bedroom only), I try to imagine what Roger would think of it as a potential home. He is a useful yardstick (if you'll pardon the phrase), because he is fairly particular and needs to be close to a railway station.

If you are looking for a family home to let, it might help to imagine what the children might think or whether mum will be comfortable with the layout of the kitchen. One good tip if you are buying a family house is that a separate utility room is always a bonus.

Anyway, view with caution and don't be swayed by the agent's selling technique. Take your list with you and make notes as you view, because after you've seen three or four, they all start to merge together. I make brief notes such as: bedroom OK, needs painting; new floors throughout; replace shower head; new taps needed; lounge too small.

Here is a checklist of questions to ask the agents as you are viewing.

CHECKLIST

Is this a good area for letting? ☐

What else is let in this street? ☐

If I spend £2,000 on modernising the kitchen and bathroom, what sort of rental could be achieved? ☐

What could I get for it if I leave it as it is? ☐

Where is the nearest bus stop? ☐

What sort of people live in this area? ☐

Should I furnish it? ☐

What are the service charges? ☐

How long has it been on the market? ☐

Will the vendors take a lower offer? ☐

The agent should be able to answer all these and more, so don't be afraid to put him on the spot. Some agents are extremely helpful and will even predict what your annual rental will be and therefore your yield. As with buying any property, always check the heating and the plumbing, etc. I usually test the shower to see what the water pressure is like.

Here is a checklist of questions to ask yourself after the viewing.

CHECKLIST

Is the property in the right location for letting? ☐

Have I asked all the right questions? ☐

Does it need a survey? ☐

Does it meet my criteria? ☐

Is the building sound? ☐

Is it fairly priced? ☐

Do the sums work out in my favour? ☐

Have I taken any useful measurements? ☐

Have I checked the plumbing and heating? ☐

How much do I need to budget for refurbishment? ☐

Do I need to view it again at a different time of day? ☐

This last question is quite important. It may be wise to view the property after office hours because a locale can change dramatically when the children are home from school and everyone is back from work. Can you park? Is it noisy? These may be irritant factors that prevent you from successfully letting your property. However, if you are catering to the student market, these issues are hardly likely to affect its potential.

Newspaper advertisements

The newspapers are a terrific source of properties to buy, both through estate agents' advertisements and private ads placed by vendors. Read them carefully and dismiss any that do not meet your criteria. When something catches your eye, ring up and ask all the questions that I listed earlier, making notes as you go. If it sounds ideal, make an appointment to view; don't wait for them to send you the details because you could be losing precious time. If, on the other hand, it sounds marginal, you can always get back to them later.

The internet

The same goes for the internet. At the back of this book are many website addresses that provide hours of fun while you trawl through looking for the perfect investment. Do not despair though, because this is fast becoming the way to buy and sell and when you get bored you can always look at all those castles in Spain!

> If you are female and are viewing a property that has been advertised privately, either on the internet or in the press, always take a friend with you – for obvious reasons.

Buying at auction

Another way of finding a property is to buy it at an auction. I have never gone down this route but I have been to several property auctions. They can be quite scary but the main thing is to be prepared. Please don't be under the illusion that auctions always present a bargain because they don't. Property usually goes for its true market value but the reality is that only 'difficult' properties are sold at auction. So if you are prepared for a massive refurbishment or are seeking something with development potential, then fine.

This is how it works. Once you have found the property you want, make sure with your solicitor that the property is free of any legal problems. Often properties with title problems are those that end up being auctioned. Then you should arrange a survey if you are getting a mortgage. A number of houses with structural defects, which make it difficult to get a mortgage, are put up for auction. The lender will probably want a valuation anyway. The most important, and frightening, thing is that you must be in a position to sign the contract in the auction room and to pay the 10 per cent deposit of the purchase price there and then (the guide price is usually the seller's reserve price, so it will only go higher!).

You must then be in a position to complete the purchase on the date agreed in the contract. This is usually 28 days from the auction date, so make sure your solicitor has all the legal documents in place. Here is an auction-room checklist.

CHECKLIST

Get a loan agreed first. ☐

Decide on the property you want. ☐

Get the survey done quickly. ☐

checklist continues

Get a solicitor to check the documentation. ☐

Have 10 per cent of the guide price ready, either as a personal cheque or bankers draft. The balance will be required in 14–28 days. ☐

Know your financial limit and stick to it. ☐

Get there early so you don't miss your lot. ☐

Bring someone to support you. ☐

Buying a property that already has tenants

If the property you are interested in is already let, this should not pose a problem if the tenant has signed an Assured Shorthold Tenancy agreement. I have done this on two occasions – bought a place with a tenant already living there – and as long as all the paperwork is in order I would not advise against it.

The only problem is that in order not to inconvenience the tenants, I had to buy all the furniture and entire contents of the flat. This could work to your advantage if the furnishings are OK, but in my instance, as soon as the tenancies were over, I had to chuck everything out and start again.

Make sure all the tenant's references are in order and take over the inventory. When the tenancy agreement is over, a proper check-out report should be done to ascertain the amount of security deposit to be refunded. Of course, if he is a happy tenant you could extend his lease. The good thing about buying a property that is already let is that there is no void period at the beginning and it usually indicates that the property is desirable.

If there is no written agreement I would be wary. This could lead to complications such as eviction or non-payment. However, prior to buying the property you could put it to the tenant that you wish to have a legal agreement and see what reaction you get. Trust your instincts.

Here are some further points to note when considering buying a property that already has tenants:

- you do not pay stamp duty on the furnishings

- you buy all the contents (if it was furnished by the previous landlord)

- there will be no void period

- there should be a written agreement

- check the inventory

- do a complete check-out report at the end of the tenancy

- ask the previous landlord or lettings agent about the tenant

- check references

- check all the safety certificates.

CHAPTER 4

Buying the property

How to buy your rental property

Buying in Scotland

How to buy your rental property

The basic procedure for buying the property is the same as if you were to be an owner-occupier, except that your mortgage will be slightly different if you have a Buy to Let mortgage, and your insurance company will need to know that this is a rental property.

In a nutshell

- You've seen the property you want after doing all your research and asking all the questions.

- You put in an offer.

- Your offer is accepted.

- The agent confirms this in writing.

- You give the seller's agent your solicitor's details.

- Your finance is already in place.

- You get a survey and valuation done.

- If the survey is acceptable you should agree fixtures and fittings (e.g. Is the washing machine staying?).

- When your solicitor has completed his searches etc., he will then draw up a contract.

- You can exchange contracts with the seller and deposit your 10 per cent of the sale price in the seller's solicitor's account.

- You are now legally bound to complete the transaction. So a date will have been set for completion.

- On the completion date the property will be legally yours when the seller's solicitor has received the balance of the money.

- You will be given the keys.

There are several hidden costs involved in buying a property. They are:

- stamp duty

- mortgage arrangement fee

- legal fees (Land Registry etc.)

- conveyancing fees to your solicitor

- the survey

- council tax (until it is let)

- buildings insurance

- life assurance cover

- service charge

- removal costs (if you are furnishing)

- utility bills (until it is let).

These hidden costs must all be built into your budget and are quite separate from your mortgage loan, refurbishment costs and furnishings because they are hidden costs, meaning invisible. It may be very frustrating to think that the government get stamp duty on top of everything else, but there you are.

At present, stamp duty is:

> Nil to £60,000
> 1% to £250,000
> 3% to £500,000
> 4% over £500,001

However, stamp duty relief is available in Disadvantaged Areas on properties up to £150,000. Ask your local council planning department for details.

Negotiating

Buying a rental investment puts you in quite a strong position financially, enabling you to negotiate on the price and achieve a deal that suits *you*. Taking advice from the estate agent, you will be able to bargain with the seller because:

- you are not in a rush

- your finances are all in place

- your purchase is usually not conditional upon selling another property (i.e. no chain)

- you can offer flexibility about completion dates

- you can negotiate for extras, such as white goods, if they are useful to you.

I love negotiating but you do need to be very sensitive to the situation. For example, there is no point in putting in a low offer if there are two other people after the same property. You need to assess how desperate the seller is before you come in for the kill. If it has been on the market for some time with little interest, it is likely that the seller will take a drop in price. I usually say something like, 'If you're in a hurry I can exchange contracts next week. I'm ready, are you ready? [Meaning the paperwork.] But that's my final offer. Oh come on. [Big smile.] That's a good price in today's market.' (But I do realise this only works if you're a woman.)

Surveys

It is advisable to get a survey done before you go ahead and buy the property, because you don't want to be lumbered with a rental investment you can't let, due to damp and dry rot.

There are three types of survey you can choose:

- the homebuyer's report

- building condition survey

- full structural survey.

The homebuyer's report

This is the one that is recommended for properties less than 50 years old. Most people opt for this type of survey because it is the least expensive but it is an appraisal rather than a thorough inspection.

The building condition survey

This one offers a fuller explanation of the condition of the property and is important for older houses. The building is examined more carefully and the surveyor will produce a written report on his findings.

A full structural survey

This kind of survey is essential if your building is very old and clearly dilapidated. The surveyor should open up all areas of the house (roof joists, foundations, cavities) for extensive inspection and testing. This is more expensive but if there is much work to do, it will alert you to the areas that need immediate attention.

Surveyors

Your surveyor should be a member of the Royal Institute for Chartered Surveyors (RICS – see Useful Addresses), but always ask beforehand how much your survey will cost. Ask:

- which survey is recommended for your property and how long it will take

- for an estimate of the cost of repairs in the report

- the surveyor to organise an electrical, plumbing and heating survey from qualified firms if it is thought advisable

- if there was any asbestos on site

- how long it will be before the survey is complete (sometimes these can take up to 20 days).

Don't become emotionally involved with the building until after your survey, in case there are negative findings. You do not need the extra hassle.

CASE STUDY

An actor friend of mine bought a second flat when he was in a television series that was paying him quite well. He paid cash for it with a view to letting it out as an investment. I thought that was a bit rash as he could have got tax relief on his mortgage. Anyway, because he wasn't getting a loan he didn't need a valuation survey and decided he didn't need a building survey either. One month after the first tenant moved in, the roof caved in during a storm and the tenant had to be rehoused. The work on the roof took ages and cost a fortune and he lost rental income as well. The whole thing was a disaster. If he had had a survey done it would have highlighted the problem and he probably wouldn't have bought that flat.

CHECKLIST

Find the right property. ☐

Negotiate the price because you are in a strong position. ☐

Put in an offer. ☐

Do the sums to calculate all the hidden costs such as
stamp duty. ☐

Get a survey done. ☐

Speak to your solicitor regularly to keep on top of things. ☐

Review findings of survey. ☐

Exchange contracts. ☐

Start marketing prior to completion. ☐

Get the keys. ☐

Buying in Scotland

Buying property in Scotland is subtly different and somewhat easier than it is in England.

For example, there is no such thing as freehold or leasehold in Scotland, as most buildings are owned on 'feudal tenure', which means that they are owned outright and can be sold freely in much the same way as freehold property in England.

However, the original landowner or developer is known as the 'superior' and he can impose certain conditions on the future use of the property or land, a bit like a restrictive covenant. His consent will be required for any changes of use. Flats do not have leases and are owned, like houses, on feudal tenure. Stamp duty is also charged at a different rate.

£0–£60,000 = Nil
£60,001–£250,000 = 1%
£250,001–£500,000 = 1.5%
£500,001 upwards = 2%

Here is a summary of how you would purchase property in Scotland.

- In Scotland solicitors can act as estate agents, advertising property in local and national newspapers. They have offices that look like estate agents, but also have the staff to deal with the conveyancing and legal problems.

- The buyer only has one person to deal with.

- Solicitors can carry out their searches and enquiries very quickly because all properties are registered with a central land register, saving much time.

- The survey is done before you make an offer, and most property is freehold.

- Houses are advertised at a 'fixed price' or 'offers over' a certain price. You can't offer below.

- If the survey is satisfactory and you have arranged your finances with the lender, you can make the offer.

- The offer is made to the seller's solicitor and is legally binding once it has been accepted.

- These documents are known as 'missives' and will include the 'date of entry', which is the date you wish to take possession of your home.

- Once the 'missives' have been concluded, your solicitor will be sent the title deeds of the property.

- If everything is OK and searches turn up nothing too alarming, a document called 'the disposition' will be drawn up transferring the property to you.

- You give your solicitor the money and the solicitor arranges for the whole purchase price, including any mortgage, to be transferred to the seller's solicitor.

- You receive the keys on the 'date of entry' along with the disposition.

CHAPTER 5

Preparing your property for the rental market

The turnaround

Furnished or unfurnished?

Regulations and safety

Decorating inside and out

Which end of the market?

The turnaround

The turnaround is the time between buying a property and renting it out or between one tenant leaving and another moving in. It is also known as a void period (i.e. no money coming in) or down time.

The trick is to have as quick a turnaround as possible so that you have money coming into the bank to cover your costs. If you have an empty property that isn't ready to let and your builders have disappeared, this will turn into a nightmare scenario, so here is how to avoid it.

Be prepared

I'm going to be honest. You *must* be prepared and organised and make lists of things you can do in advance to cut down the turnaround time.

When you have exchanged contracts on the property (and only then because anything could go wrong during the conveyancing process), you can start alerting your builder, plasterer, electrician, plumber, flooring specialist, etc. as to your completion date, when you would like work to commence.

Of course, you may be doing it all yourself or you may have no refurbishment necessary, in which case you only need to find the tenant, and can start advertising immediately with the date of completion as the commencement of the tenancy. If you are using a letting agent, they will need to see the flat before marketing can begin.

If the property is still occupied, ask the owner or agent if you can spend time taking measurements and perhaps showing the property to your carpenter, plumber, etc. This will help enormously because you and they can start ordering materials for the job. You may need bathroom suites, tiles, timber, kitchen units, light fittings, etc. and all these will need to be ordered. It isn't like popping into B&Q and grabbing a tin of paint!

If the property is vacant it will make life much easier because you can collect the keys from the agent and make all the necessary notes, measurements and plans at your leisure.

Confirm with your tradespeople when you would like them to start and order all the materials to be delivered on a certain date. If you are having floors laid, or carpets fitted, arrange for estimates and fittings, and measure up for fridges, washing machines and dryers.

Basic upgrade

Even if you are doing a very basic upgrade, it still pays to be well prepared. Making lists is a life-saver for me, otherwise I would go mad. I have to admit, it gets easier each time I do it but I still make mistakes. Once you have a completion date, you can start planning and should be able to get a tenant ensconced within a week!

I bought a property once that didn't need very much done to it and, with forward planning, I turned it around really quickly.

- I booked my decorators.

- Booked the electrician.

- Bought paint and chrome door handles.

- Bought contemporary light fittings.

- Booked flooring to be fitted.

- Booked cleaners.

- Booked an inventory clerk.

- Instructed letting agent to let it from 12 September

On 5 September – completion day – the property was stripped of old carpets etc.

On 6 and 7 September, the decorators painted the whole flat white. Emulsion on the walls, eggshell on all woodwork.

On 8 September the wood flooring was fitted.

On 9 September the cleaners went in and did a thorough professional clean. I went in to hang blinds and curtains, and a handyman fitted my new lighting, door handles and a huge mirror that had been specially cut for the bathroom.

On 10 September furniture and washing machine were delivered.

On 11 September I dressed the flat and dashed around buying light bulbs etc.

On 12 September the inventory and check-in report was done and the tenant moved in.

Now admittedly this sounds very smug and it isn't always as easy as that, but it can be done.

(By the way, don't forget the Gas Safety Certificate, which should be done prior to a tenant moving in.)

The postscript to this particular property was that the chap who rented it (a young university lecturer) had a very attractive girlfriend. She used to wear impossibly high heels and would clip-clop around on my wood floors at all hours. Apparently, they would come in at 2 a.m., going clip-clop, clip-clop, bang the doors and have a row until 3 a.m.

The other residents of the flats were, naturally, not amused by these antics and the people below were particularly unimpressed with her high heels, so I received a complaint. I spoke to the tenant and he promised they wouldn't bang the doors any more and she would remove her heels.

Two weeks later, I received another complaint because they had lost their keys and were pressing all the buzzers at 2 a.m. asking to be let in! This is not acceptable behaviour, so I was asked to get them to leave.

The tenant pleaded that he had just split with his clip-clopping girlfriend and would be really quiet, but I insisted and he was really good about it.

CHECKLIST

After exchange of contracts, get access to the property to take measurements. ☐

Measure windows, floors, kitchen area and anything that needs refurbishment. ☐

Take *lots* of notes on the state of property. ☐

Call builder or plumber, etc. to confirm dates and list of works. Arrange for them to view and do estimates. ☐

Contact letting agent to prime them as to approximately when the property will be ready. ☐

If not using an agent plan advertising (see page 92). ☐

Start ordering materials, such as tiles or anything that has a long lead time. ☐

Make list of *everything* required, down to the number of door handles or light switches. ☐

Get estimates for flooring. ☐

checklist continues

Start ordering furniture (if you are going to furnish, most of it needs ordering). ☐

Arrange an inventory clerk – if necessary. ☐

Book cleaners and window cleaners. ☐

Renovating the property

There are two schools of thought regarding whether one should spend enormous amounts of money and energy renovating a property prior to putting it on the rental market. One is that it is time-consuming and costly to start renovating a property when all you really want to do is get it on the market and ready to let as quickly as possible. The second school of thought, to which I personally subscribe, is that buying a property that requires some renovation and refurbishment, not only enhances the capital growth of the property but also its potential letability to the sort of tenant I am aiming to attract. Over the last 10 years I have usually bought, with one exception, an old property in need of updating (i.e. a new kitchen and bathroom), that I can then redecorate to appeal to my target market (which, as discussed before, is 30-something young professionals who require a certain level of style and comfort). I have gone down the rather tortuous route of getting in builders and doing a turnaround as quickly as possible in order to get it on to the market, aware of the fact that every week during the renovations is a void period with no rental income.

However, once the renovation is complete I have a property that should be able to fulfil all market demands for the next 10 years. This is not to say that it will not need redecorating, as it will. I usually redecorate every three to four years and sometimes at the end of each tenancy, depending on the level of wear and tear. If you want to attract a top end client the property always has to be presented in absolutely tip-top condition. That means no scuff marks and no chipped furniture. Of course, in an ideal world, buying a property that is ready to move into is the ultimate solution for the landlord because immediately upon completion you can start letting the property and getting a return on your investment.

So, I can see the other side of the argument. However, buying a property like that will probably be more expensive and it all depends on your budget. A rapid turnaround is essential if you are to increase your profit margins (see page 140).

CHECKLIST

Modernise kitchen. ☐

Modernise bathroom. ☐

Redecorate throughout. ☐

Install good quality fixtures and fittings. ☐

Install wood flooring in most rooms. ☐

Carpets in the bedroom. ☐

Ceramic tiles in the bathroom. ☐

Furnished or unfurnished?

My flats are all fully furnished because of the type of tenant I am aiming to attract. They need flexibility within their professions, so even though they may own the latest hi-fi equipment, they don't own any furniture. They want to be able to move straight in with their personal possessions and not have to worry about finding a bed.

I think property always looks better when it is fully dressed as some tenants have no imagination, so it is good to present the property as if it were ready for immediate occupation.

When the new Fire and Furnishings Regulations were brought in (in 1988), the market saw a turnaround with more landlords preferring to let their properties unfurnished, because of all the hassle with changing curtains, sofas and mattresses to comply with the new regulations. (Be careful when buying furniture at auction, as I do, because some items just don't comply with the regulations.)

The demand for furnished flats has now diminished, with 50 per cent of the rental market being for unfurnished property. The landlord needs to be very flexible and even though the demand is for unfurnished you should always show the property fully furnished. This gives the tenant a proper feel for the ambience of the property and, believe it or not, a furnished room with sensible-sized furniture will look bigger than an unfurnished one. Problems still tend to arise when dealing with Americans, though, who often have larger pieces of furniture that do not fit easily into smaller English homes. So they may decide to take the flat furnished and put everything of their own in storage.

Most large family houses will be rented unfurnished, with everything being shipped over from abroad. However, you still need to furnish it, just in case. This can be a real pain, I know, as storage is expensive but of course your rent will reflect that. However, by showing it furnished the tenant may decide to keep several pieces, including beds, and you won't have to get rid of much.

Also, there is much demand for homes for those who are between selling and buying. Again 50 per cent will want the property furnished because it is far less hassle to put everything into storage, and 50 per cent will want it unfurnished because they are not sure how long they are going to be there and they want their possessions with them. Storage is pricey and people want their home comforts. So, flexibility is the key word here.

Here is a quick summary to help you decide whether to go for furnished or unfurnished:

- Student lets will need to be furnished.

- Lower end will probably want the let unfurnished.

- Middle market could be either: 50 per cent require unfurnished but you must show it furnished.

- Upper end – professional. If the let's in the city, probably furnished, but could go either way.

- Upper end – family home. Usually unfurnished.

The moral is: be flexible.

CASE STUDY

Thomas Greene was a mean sort of landlord, always trying to cut corners and save money. His furniture was cheap and his mattresses had not been changed in years, resulting in a lumpy, uncomfortable night's sleep. His tenants did not renew their contract after six months and moved elsewhere. This cost him more in void periods and turnaround fees. Remember, by providing good quality furniture you will enhance your chances of keeping your tenants for longer.

Always leave a smart folder containing instructions, guarantees and advice for operating everything such as the cooker, washing machine, shower, central heating, etc., and giving the whereabouts of meters (gas and electricity) and stopcocks for the water supply.

What to provide

I have found that it makes economic sense to buy good quality furnishings and white goods. They last longer and cause less hassle. With careful forward planning, a deal can be struck at some retail outlets or with manufacturers if you are buying in quantity. So, rather than buying a fridge one week and a washing machine the next, make a list of all the white goods you need, such as fridge-freezer, washing machine, dryer, dishwasher (if necessary), and go to a reputable supplier who will give you a favourable price for a multiple purchase.

The same could be said for items such as vacuum cleaner, toaster, kettle, etc., which could all be purchased from the same supplier.

This is what I usually put in my flats:

CHECKLIST

Sofas and armchairs (sometimes a sofa bed for visiting guests). ☐

A table and chairs for dining (depending on space this could be a foldaway table). ☐

Heating. ☐

Beds with good quality mattresses. ☐

Chest of drawers and wardrobe. ☐

Pillows. ☐

Lamps and mirrors. ☐

Cooker. ☐

Fridge and freezer. ☐

Washer/drying machine. ☐

Kettle. ☐

Toaster. ☐

Microwave oven. ☐

Vacuum cleaner. ☐

Complete set of kitchen utensils. ☐

Complete set of crockery and cutlery (enough for four). ☐

Set of glasses (four tall glasses, wine glasses and tumblers). ☐

Set of saucepans. ☐

Iron and ironing board. ☐

Curtains or blinds. ☐

Side tables and a coffee table. ☐

Most landlords are not obliged to supply televisions and video equipment but I have found that providing a wide-screen TV and DVD player gives the property an extra 'wow' factor, particularly in difficult times when a tenant can be hard to find. However, it is entirely up to you how far you want to go. In the early days when I was a fledgling landlord I used to furnish my flats with antiques, full bed linen and crystal glasses only to find that my generosity inevitably ended in tears. If you have any prized possessions they do not belong in a rental property.

You do not have to supply the following:

- towels
- bed linen

- TV, video or DVD

- duvets

- special kitchen equipment (although a girlfriend of mine always provides a cappuccino machine!).

Any fabric that is used in the property should be fairly hardwearing, durable and flame retardent. There are many good quality fabrics, which will look gorgeous, but which also provide sturdy upholstery. I use damasks, heavy cotton and linen, chenille and woven fabric on the furniture, and plain cottons for the curtains. Keep the colours very neutral.

Regulations and safety

Legal requirements

There are legal requirements to which a landlord is obliged to adhere. They cover electrical safety, gas safety and fire resistance.

Electrical equipment

It is recommended that all electrical equipment and appliances should be checked annually for safety and have the correct fuses fitted. All wiring circuits and sockets must be checked at the start of a let and regularly after that. Some letting agents are more particular about having safety certificates than others, but it is in your best interests to ensure that all electrical appliances are properly fitted and safe. They should be inspected by an NICEIC (National Inspection Council for Electrical Installation Contracting – see Useful Addresses) contractor. I keep my electrical items to a minimum simply because it means there are fewer things to go wrong. There won't be a certificate issued to you by the NICEIC, but an inspection will cover you if any appliances were to harm your tenants or their friends.

Gas safety

The Gas Safety (Installation and Use) Regulations 1998 state that a landlord is responsible for having the gas pipework and appliances certified as being in good working order. This should cover gas oven, boiler, central heating and gas fires, if any, and gas meters.

A Gas Safety Certificate is a government requirement and your agent will need to hold a copy in their office. These are quite expensive but prove that the boiler and all appliances are sound. They need to be renewed every year, not just at the start of a tenancy and must be issued by a tradesperson who is registered with the Council for Registered Gas Installers (CORGI – see Useful Addresses).

> If you do not get one of these certificates and your tenant suffers from carbon monoxide poisoning, you could face a huge fine and even imprisonment.

Fire resistance

Unless you comply with the Furniture and Furnishings (Fire and Safety) Regulations 1988 you could be fined up to £5,000. All upholstery, curtains, mattresses and sofas have to pass certain flammability tests and must be thus labelled. Any furniture bought after 1990 will automatically comply with these fire regulations, but be careful when buying furniture at auctions, because if it predates 1990 it will not necessarily comply.

Smoke detectors

The Department of the Environment introduced new regulations requiring any new building (built after June 1992) to have smoke detectors installed. If your property is older than this they recommend that battery-operated detectors be installed on each floor. Always change the batteries at the beginning of each tenancy.

Negligence and personal injury

As a landlord it is your duty to provide a safe home for your tenant and anyone else who enters your property. If they can prove that you were negligent in any way, you could be sued and ordered to pay damages. So if, for example, there is an incident involving the gas boiler and one of your tenants suffers a personal injury and the Gas Safety Certificate is out of date you would be liable for damages.

Insurance

You will need to provide insurance to cover you against certain risks. The main policies are as follows:

- Buildings insurance – this will cover the property against fire, water damage, vandalism, weather damage, etc.

- Contents insurance – this will cover items such as carpets, fixtures and fittings and any furniture that you have provided for your tenant.

- Rental guarantee – this will insure against your tenant defaulting on the rental payments.

- Emergency assistance – this will cover the costs of any emergency repairs that have to be carried out. I do not take out this insurance personally but some letting agents recommend it.

Always remember to tell the truth when filling out your forms and if you have had any previous claims you must reveal them. Any untruths or discrepancies will immediately negate any claims that you may make. Insurance companies are notoriously tricky about paying out and if they catch you fibbing you may find it difficult to get insurance in the future.

Decorating inside and out

Decorating your rental property must be kept as simple and as unfussy as possible. I know to my cost that letting my own taste get in the way can prove an expensive exercise. Just because I happen to like rich colours doesn't mean that everybody will and decorating my first rental property with terracotta walls and black granite surfaces everywhere meant that I was reducing my target market by approximately 80 per cent.

The key is to decorate your property to appeal to the widest possible market, so the most important word here is *neutral*. I now paint all the walls off-white or a pale creamy colour, the floors are pale wood or sandy-coloured carpet, the kitchen units are white, the bathroom tiles are white. You get the picture? This way when your potential tenant is viewing the property there is nothing that can be taken exception to.

Fixtures and fittings should be of the highest quality, but keep them simple. For example, no corner baths; an ordinary pressed steel bath will suffice. No frilly curtains. No patterned wallpaper. No fluffy loo-seat cover. (God forbid!) The water pressure must be excellent. Preparing your property for the rental market is much the same as preparing a property to sell. How it is presented to the viewer is all important. (A bare mattress can look very unappealing, so I always cover them with an attractive throw.)

- Keep it simple.

- Keep it neutral.

- Keep it clean.

Which end of the market?

Middle market

The biggest demand is for flats in the mid-range. These usually appeal to single professionals or young couples who have yet to buy. They are normally well situated and well appointed. So, let's look at the middle market first. Supposing you've found a nice one-bedroom flat in a great location close to all the amenities. What should it look like?

I have found that the more neutral everything is, the more successful it will be. Neutrality can't offend anybody. The secret is to make it look carefully thought out without being too designer conscious. Buy one or two really good pieces of furniture to lend the flat an air of class, such as a glass coffee table and large gilt mirror. They are both practical and mirrors help to open up the space.

Lighting is really important, too, especially if it is quite a small flat. I use downlighters and wall lights quite a bit and spotlights in the kitchen.

- The kitchen should be neutral or white with maybe coloured tiles. Avoid a very modern statement kitchen as it will date very quickly. Cream tiles look great but a deep green or blue could add a nice contrast. I equip mine fully with crockery and cutlery, but you could take advice on this. A good oven with separate hob is advisable because old-fashioned kitchens are out. If there is no room for both a washer and a dryer then a washer-dryer will do. Make sure your tenant has all the instructions on how everything operates and make sure all appliances are serviced regularly.

- The bathroom should have a white suite with power shower. (You will need to install a separate pressure pump, if the water pressure isn't up to it.) I usually tile the whole bathroom, which is expensive but it saves redecorating every few years as steam plays havoc with paper or paint. You can buy fabulous large (12 x 8 in) tiles that look like marble and use ceramic tiles on the floor. Most people hate shower curtains so if you can install a glass shower screen then great. If not, change the curtain after each tenancy as they usually look revolting after a bit of use. If you have room for a separate shower cubicle, that's even better. The bath taps should be mixer taps with a cradle shower attachment. All the taps and accessories should be in the very best chrome but not too modern as these will date. I use a very classic design.

- The toilet should be low level with a wooden loo seat – don't ask me why, it just looks better – and bidets are no longer a requirement and are an unnecessary expense. I always put a large mirror in the bathroom to double the space and for practical reasons too.

- The bedroom should have plenty of cupboards, and if you are furnishing it (see page 69, Furnished or Unfurnished?) should have two bedside tables, a chest of drawers, mirror, a double bed with a good mattress and neutral carpet.

- The rest of the flat, hallway and sitting room, should be as neutral as possible but with very good furniture. I always provide pictures on the walls but tenants want to hang their own, that's fine by me. (The contract stipulates, though, that the flat must be reinstated on hand-over.) I feel that the flat should be presented in such a way that the tenant feels immediately at home and wants to move in straight away, but do not over-accessorise.

If professional cleaners have been in after the tenancy, you will need to remove all those bits of silver foil they put under furniture feet. I would also make the bed and change the light bulbs etc. One hour of titivating can make all the difference.

To get 'The Look'

- Neutral decor throughout the flat. I use soft creams on the walls and off-white woodwork.

- Stripped wooden floors, in the hall, kitchen and sitting room. This is a current fad and may not be appropriate in some circumstances.

- Bathroom in white with chrome accessories.

- Power shower in the bathroom.

- Tiles, laminate or vinyl flooring in bathroom.

- Neutral unfussy curtains (although bamboo blinds are popular at the moment).

- Good quality lighting. Spotlights, lamps, downlighters.

- Kitchen should be modern, bright, well lit and well equipped with a dishwasher, ceramic hob, microwave, washer-dryer, etc.

- Carpet in the bedroom.

- Fitted wardrobes in the bedroom and lots of storage elsewhere if possible.

- Furniture must be sturdy and of good quality. Modern, light and bright.

- A dining table with four chairs should be in the main living area. If there is no room, maybe a foldaway table.

- A desk or work space.

CASE STUDY

My girlfriend Caroline let her flat when she went to work in America and had a full inventory prepared. However, in the flat was a beautiful chest of drawers that she had been left by her granny. When she returned to live in the flat, she discovered that the furniture had been badly marked and the deposit wasn't enough to cover the cost of repairing it. She really should have removed the chest of drawers and any other precious items before letting her flat.

Lower end

If you are aiming at the lower end of the market, it means your tenant will have different requirements and this affects the way you present the property. Some tenants can be fairly heavy on furniture and appliances so you need to provide robust items.

A tenant on a tight budget is not going to be so fussy or demanding about decor. If you decide not to furnish this will help keep costs down and also provide less potential for damages. The property should be bright and freshly painted throughout in white. It is the cheapest colour to buy and easy to redo when necessary. Use a vinyl silk on the walls as it is easier to wash down than emulsion, and eggshell on the woodwork. I would put a hardwearing industrial carpet throughout the property in a sort of flecked grey colour. This hides the dirt and stains but still looks good. Laying wood flooring in this case would be an unnecessary expense.

The bathroom and kitchen will still need to be presentable but not necessarily up to the minute.

To get 'The Look'

- White paint throughout.

- Hardwearing carpet.

- Ask advice as to whether it should be furnished.

- Robust appliances.

CASE STUDY

Brian Hampton bought a flat that needed total modernisation with a view to letting it to the council for rehousing applicants. Unfortunately he let his budget run away with him by installing the sort of kitchen that he had dreamed of, instead of something a lot more practical and hardwearing. It took some serious bashing and he was asked to replace it. If he had installed a kitchen that had cost a quarter of the price, he would have saved himself a lot of time and added expense.

Letting to students

Once again, everything in the property will need to be fairly sturdy to withstand the kind of wear and tear that a group of 20-year-olds can inflict. However, students are taking more care of their property these days, according to several agents I spoke to, and require good quality appliances. This is where it is false economy to buy cheaper white goods because they get such heavy use. A good washing machine, dryer, microwave, fridge, dishwasher even, will last longer.

Students require furnished accommodation and are becoming fairly demanding style-wise. If you want the better class of student, he won't want brown 1950s furniture and a Formica kitchen. I suggest you paint the whole place white and have pale, unfussy blinds. If the floors can be stripped wood with rugs that would be desirable, if not, heavy duty carpet in a dark colour will do the job. Students like heavy, chunky furniture, which is contemporary, and it needs to be hardwearing. There are several mail order companies that I use who make good quality furniture at a bargain price. Buy sofas with loose covers, in a dark colour, that are easy to wash. They will need a dining table and chairs as well, and most bedrooms should have double beds.

If you can install a separate shower as well as one in the main bathroom this will be a plus factor. They will need a separate loo too.

To make things simpler you could draw up the contract with one student whom you put in charge. Prepare a detailed inventory, ask for a deposit up front and arrange a direct debit for the rent.

To get 'The Look'

- Paint the whole place white.

- Good plumbing is essential.

- Install a fire alarm.

- Buy good quality appliances – washing machine, separate dryer, fridge, microwave, dishwasher and vacuum cleaner.

- Use heavy duty carpet and simple curtains/blinds.

- Buy sofas and chairs with loose covers in a dark colour.

- Buy good, sturdy furniture because it will get heavy wear.

- Provide a dining table and chairs.

- Install a separate shower.

- Bedrooms should have double beds.

- Kitchen must be fully equipped.

- Prepare an inventory.

CASE STUDY

Kirsty Frogmoreton was really looking forward to going up to university and was determined to find somewhere nice to live with her three girlfriends. She and her mother looked at several places but they all seemed rather bland and a bit boyish. Eventually they found a terraced house that had been recently modernised and had some really funky furniture. But the best bit was this really awesome walk-in shower and the main bathroom was really well thought out. Also, each room had its own desk, which Kirsty thought was a bonus. So, even though they were paying a bit more rent, Kirsty and her friends felt it was worth it.

Upper end

If you own a property that falls within the upper end of the rental market, your potential tenant is going to expect a certain level of furnishings and decor. With the higher rent comes higher expectations.

With its smart location, or exceptional size, it will need to be exquisitely decorated. This sort of property appeals to the corporate tenant on a company let, but the downside is that the void periods may well be longer. In big cities your tenant is likely to be a visiting executive from a foreign company, or bank, over here with his wife and family.

They usually require a parking space and you must be linked up to all the latest technology. Some of them like a cleaner provided or even accommodation for a live-in housekeeper.

If you are aiming at this market, take advice from your letting agent on what is required. The interior decoration needs to be of the very highest standard and can be quite luxurious. The colours don't have to be completely neutral but steer away from strong ones. Americans love big, spacious bathrooms with power showers and they love antiques. I used the auction rooms a lot to furnish the bigger flats and have bought tapestry wall-hangings and a mahogany dining table with eight chairs. They will normally require one or two reception rooms for entertaining and at least two bathrooms.

I have found that young and wealthy executives usually like a very clean, linear style so stay away from anything too traditional and soft. When furnishing an upper end property the quality will have to follow right through to the linen, crockery and cutlery. For these rentals, the tenant expects crystal, not glass.

In London, Americans love apartments in those old mansion blocks with panelled hallways and marble floors. They love the whole 'Englishness' of it all. They are also very security-conscious so any property that has secure parking, entry-phones, gates, porterage and video cameras is a plus. Of course, the service charges are very high in apartments like that, so remember to take that into account when doing your sums.

To get 'The Look'

- Decor should be quietly elegant.

- Fixtures and fittings must be of a very high standard.

- Bathrooms should be spacious, with no carpet.

- Good fabrics essential.

- Must have parking.

- If furnished, go for quality.

- Must have space for entertaining.

- Kitchen should be fabulous.

- Security essential. Porterage a plus.

- If it's a family home, out of town, must be near good rail links and schools.

One of the best tips I was ever given by an agent was to remember that when couples are viewing it is usually, 90 per cent of the time, the woman who will make the final decision. Women notice good quality curtains and soft furnishings and are more impressed by the quality of the kitchen and bathroom. Men are generally more influenced by factors that will make a statement about their standing – the price, the location – whereas women are influenced by comfort and style.

Also, women tend to procrastinate far less than men, which helps in the rental market. If you offer them the right look, they'll say 'Great. When can I move in?', whereas a chap will say 'I'll just see six more.'

CHAPTER 6

Letting the property

Long lets versus short lets

Finding the tenant

The Assured Shorthold Tenancy

Letting your property through an agent

Managing the property

Letting your property in Scotland

Long lets versus short lets

A quiet, tidy tenant, on a four-year let, who pays on time, is my idea of landlord heaven. Long lets have always been my preference because they are far less traumatic. Short lets or, worse, holiday lets (see Chapter 10, Investing in the Holiday Rental Market) have such a rapid turnaround that I couldn't possibly manage them myself and I would need an army of cleaners and decorators.

There is now an increased demand for short lets due to the need for flexibility among some employees. Tourism also plays a part in the need for good short lets due to a preference by some visitors for home comforts and self-catering facilities in our major cities. Amazingly, yields of up to 20 per cent are now achievable, due to the huge demand from corporate tenants and holidaymakers.

For example, an upper end corporate flat renting for £400 a week on a long-term basis could fetch as much as £650 a week on a short let. That would include gas and electricity, and you would be expected to provide all the latest technology, plus maid and laundry service. They become serviced apartments really.

So, if you have a furnished flat in a very good location, very central to all amenities and with a very high specification finish, it may be worth considering short lets. (A short let is considered to be anything from a week to three months.)

However, the high turnover of tenants will cause greater maintenance costs and more damages. Your insurance will go up (be sure to inform your insurance company or else they may well refuse to pay any claim) and the agent's commission will be higher.

For example:

10% commission becomes 15% for 3 months or less

12.5% commission becomes 17.5% for 3 months or less

15% commission becomes 20% or 21% for 3 months or less

The void periods between short lets can be longer and the stress will be greater I'm sure, and your other costs will be incurred more frequently, like cleaning, tenancy agreements and inventories. So you need to do the sums carefully and see if it is really worth it. Personally, I think short lets are a lot of hassle for a marginally more substantial financial gain.

Short lets	**Long lets**
higher yield *but*	lower yield *but*
greater maintenance costs	less maintenance
higher insurance	lower insurance
higher commission	lower commission
longer voids	shorter voids

CASE STUDY

Robin Doughty decided to go for short lets in his designer pad in central Leeds. Having heard that there were several local companies using flats instead of hotels for their visiting executives, he installed Broadband and all the other technical wizardry he could think of and placed it with a specialist agency. They took him to see some of the other flats on their books to show him what he was up against and he was stunned to see the high level of decoration, the fresh flowers, the Egyptian cotton sheets, the plasma screens and the limestone bathrooms. He immediately implemented some changes and marketed it privately on the internet and now has a regular turnover of clients. He realised that to compete you have to invest.

Letting your home out for short lets

If the whole family are vacating your property for a two- or three-week holiday – if you live alone it is even simpler – you could consider letting your home on a short-term basis. Whether it is a flat in the middle of a city or a family house in a rural retreat, there are several companies nationwide who specialise in letting out a home in this way. However, it is quite complicated and requires some effort and not a little upheaval. The financial return can be considerable but here are some things you need to think about *before* you start emptying your wardrobes:

- check that it is permitted under the terms of your lease, by the local authority or by your mortgage company

- you will need to inform your insurance company and may need to take out extra cover

- you will need to comply with the gas, electrical and fire safety regulations

- all your furnishings and upholstered items will need to be fire-resistant and labelled in order to comply with fire safety regulations

- lock up valuables and store any rare and precious antiques

- the property should be clean and tidy

- empty wardrobes and drawers

- have an inventory taken.

If you use a short let company they will advise you on presentation and what to provide. This is your home though and not a holiday let so I strongly urge you to go through the proper channels and get the right contracts drawn up. Be prepared for upheaval when you return as a lot of things will have moved to different places. However, if it is successful and you do this often, you will find that it will change the way you live for ever. (You'll acquire less clutter.)

Company lets

I've been lucky enough in the past to let my flats to a company or corporation, which pay the rent instead of the tenant, hence the term company let. Under the terms of the agreement, the company can accommodate one of their employees – or indeed a whole family – in your property and take the responsibility for the tenancy. This is ideal for many reasons because:

- the agreement is usually a long let

- void periods are minimised

- the rent always gets paid

- they may agree to undertake some maintenance

- the tenant is usually not bothersome.

However, companies are very fussy about accommodation and usually only go for the upper end of the market and require extra things like space for entertaining and all the latest technology. They also prefer to deal with an agent and not directly with the landlord as they feel this keeps it on a more professional basis. So if you have a good quality, top of the range, self-contained, cutting-edge, fully managed property, complete with all technical facilities, a company let would be just perfect.

Finding the tenant

Finding the tenant without an agent

Personally, I always use a letting agent to find my tenant and take on the responsibility of checking references etc. However, a lot of landlords prefer to do it themselves and save the extra 10 per cent. This is risky because as soon as a problem arises it is up to the landlord to deal with it, whereas an agent can act as a barrier, an interface. Before you decide to go it alone, are you sure you have enough time available to do the work of an agent? You must be realistic about this because the longer your property is empty the more it is going to cost you.

Doing it yourself

Start advertising for a tenant as soon as possible – even before the completion date, if your property is ready for immediate occupation.

- Advertise in the local press.

- Advertise on the internet.

- Contact local organisations or large companies' human resources (HR) departments.

- Contact the local council.

Local press

This is probably the most straightforward way of finding a tenant. Make your advertisement as precise and clear as possible in order to stop time-wasters. For example, if it is suitable for several young people as opposed to a professional couple, then say so, e.g. 'Would suit four students'. You will need to include in your details:

- The area – just because the ad is in the local paper doesn't necessarily mean it is in the same area. Be specific.

- The size of the property – the number of bedrooms, kitchen, bathroom, separate shower, etc. Does it have a large lounge-dining area?

- Whether it is furnished or not – this will make a difference.

- The price – you could put this at the top if you feel it is competitively priced. It is usually quoted per calender month – e.g. £400 p.c.m. – but a fairly neat trick is to quote it weekly, so that the rent seems lower than others.

- Any special features – such as a garage or garden.

- Contact details – your telephone numbers and your name.

The internet

This is becoming an essential tool for all marketing and if you place an honestly worded ad, you should receive a great deal of interest. Some of the sites are free and some will charge a one-off payment. Shop around. (For site addresses see Useful Websites.)

Local organisations

It is always worth trying any local companies which employ a lot of people. Give the HR department printed details of the property available and call them every week to remind them that you are still available.

Local council

The council will have lists of people looking for accommodation and if you are prepared to let to them (unemployed, refugees or asylum seekers), you should write to the housing department with your details.

If you are determined to let the property yourself, it is important to deal with people with whom you can communicate easily. For example, if you are uncomfortable with unemployed people or refugees (there could be a language barrier), don't aim your marketing in that direction. If you like dealing with single professionals, as I do, then steer your search likewise. If you have done your research and chosen a target market as mentioned before, you should find your tenant easily.

Interviewing the tenant

Once your advertisements start to appear, the phone will be ringing (hopefully) with people anxious to know whether the property is still available.

Interview them carefully over the phone before agreeing to let them view, because you may find they are not suitable for your type of property. You may wish to have a list of questions ready such as:

Q Is his job temporary or permanent?

Q What does he earn?

Q How long has he been in that job?

Q Where was he living before?

Q Why did he move?

Q Could he provide a guarantor?

Q Is he aware of all the costs involved in renting your place (i.e. council tax, phone bill, electricity, gas etc.)?

Q How long does he think he'll be renting for?

Q Who will actually be living in the property (girlfriend, dog, etc.)?

Q Does he smoke?

Take his name and telephone number and tell him you will call back to arrange a time for viewing or, if you think this applicant is unsuitable, tell him so in as nice a way as possible. There is no point wasting his time and yours, so it is better to be up front about it.

You will also need to provide information over the phone that is a great deal more detailed than in the advertisement. Remember, the tenant is probably ringing several places, so in a way you are being interviewed too! You need the right tenant, so as well as asking questions you will need to answer several. Be prepared. Have in front of you everything he might need to know.

CASE STUDY

Mike Baron placed his advertisement with his telephone numbers at the bottom, but on his home number he didn't have an answerphone and some people didn't want to ring his mobile, so he missed several potential tenants. He should only have included the number where he was most available.

Checklist – property information to give the tenant

Accommodation

1 double bedroom	Queen-size bed
Lounge	Dining table and chairs
Kitchen	Recently refurbished
Bathroom	With separate shower
Hallway	Large storage cupboard

Facilities fully furnished with:
automatic washing machine

electric hob and oven
fridge
microwave oven
telephone
electric storage heating

Rent
£525 per calendar month, payable on 1st of month
Electricity, telephone, water, council tax are extra
£600 deposit required

Lease
1 year minimum
Available 1st July
No pets
References required

Features
Free car parking space

You will very quickly be able to tell which applicants are going to be suitable from a process of elimination based on the answers you get. Your instincts can play a major part too. Even though I use an agent, if my instincts about a tenant ring alarm bells, I ask the agent to keep marketing it and not to accept that tenant.

Preparing for the viewing

Arrange for the various suitable applicants to view the property at half-hourly intervals, if they are all coming on the same day. This will give you plenty of time to show them around, ask all the questions and have a breather before the next one.

Before they arrive, prepare the flat/house so that it is presented in the best possible way. Whether it is a student flat or a large family house, it is attention to detail that matters if you are keen to secure the best tenant. These days, supply outstrips demand, so the tenant can be extremely choosy. This is more prevalent in the upper end of the rental market, admittedly, but it is still important.

So, first impressions count. The following checklist will remind you what you need to do.

CHECKLIST

Checklist for presenting your property at its best

Tidy up the front garden if there is one. ☐

Make sure the name or number of the house is clearly visible from the road. ☐

Remove dustbins or any rubbish that may be outside. ☐

Remove bikes, trikes and pushchairs. ☐

Clean front door. ☐

Tidy main hallway. If it is a shared residence, remove all junk mail and telephone directories (why are there always so many telephone directories in flats?). Vacuum carpet and replace any broken light bulbs. ☐

Inside the property, make sure it is warm in winter or cool in summer. ☐

Turn on lights if necessary. ☐

Tidy rooms and plump up cushions. ☐

checklist continues

Put loo seat down. ☐

Put a bedspread or throw over mattress instead of showing
bare mattress. ☐

Make sure it all smells nice. (No bad odour from bins
or drains.) ☐

Make sure you have keys if there is a bike shed, cellar, garage
or whatever to show. ☐

Have the details printed out to give to the tenant. ☐

Have all extra information to hand. ☐

SAFETY

I've mentioned this before, but I think it is a good idea to have
someone with you when you conduct the viewings – especially if
you are female. Your personal safety comes first. Never give your
home address over the phone and always check with the viewer's
place of employment.

The viewing

During the viewing, you will be able to draw potential tenants'
attention to any features you think important, but try not to 'over-
sell' the property as this can be annoying. The kitchen can be an
important factor if the tenant is female, so spend time explaining
all the appliances.

It may be worth going over the terms of the lease again, so that
there are no misunderstandings about anything, such as pets,
smoking, neighbours, etc.

The applicant may try to negotiate with you at some stage but don't be rushed into anything. You may want to see other prospective tenants first. Similarly, if you like the applicant and want to offer him the tenancy, you could indicate that, but do not make a direct offer because you need to check all references first.

Making the decision

Once you have interviewed all the applicants (I say 'all' but sometimes I'm lucky if I have one), you are in a position to decide which one is the most suitable. This could be for a variety of reasons such as financial stability, geography, employment or personality, but if none of them seem quite right, do not compromise. This could lead to discomfort and complications.

Having made the decision you will be able to offer the property to the tenant on the condition that references are acceptable and the contract has been drawn up. Sometimes a tenant will put you under pressure to move in straight away, but do not be swayed until all the paperwork is done. I would use a solicitor or an agent to draw up the contract but if you are determined to do it yourself, an Assured Shorthold Tenancy Agreement can be bought at leading stationery shops and other retail outlets or from legal publishers (for more on this see page 104).

To summarise, you will now need to:

- check the references
- draw up the Assured Shorthold Tenancy or contract
- receive a deposit.

Checking the references

Before you let anyone move into your property, you will obviously want to check that they are who they say they are, they are able to pay the rent and their references are good. The ideal situation is a company let (see page 91), because the company, the tenant's employer, is paying the rent so there is little risk of a non-payment. However, you will still need references.

- A character reference can be obtained from a previous land-lord. You need to know if he was a good tenant, if he paid on time and if he left the place in good condition.

- A financial reference should be obtained from the tenant's employer. This will show you how much the tenant earns and whether it is sufficient to cover the rent. You could also ask for a bank reference. If the tenant is from abroad or has had no previous employment, it would be wise to ask for a guarantor. This is usually a parent or guardian who will be financially responsible for the rent, if the tenant defaults on his payments.

- A credit check. My letting agents always do a credit check on the tenant, to see if they have had a consistent financial history and to see whether there are any County Court Judgments (CCJs) against them. However, a credit check is only absolutely necessary if the tenant is paying a fairly high rent and your property is well situated and therefore in demand. Note that if you are letting to students, they may not have had any credit, in which case they would fail a credit check, but this does not mean that they are uncreditworthy. They may have very nice parents who will take the financial risk. Always trust your instincts. If someone fails a credit check, it could be for a ludicrous, insignificant reason, so an employer's reference is more important.

Drawing up the contract

If you are letting without an agent you must have a proper legal agreement between you and the tenant to cover you if there are any problems in the future, such as non-payment of rent. The Assured Shorthold Tenancy should be signed by you the landlord, the tenant (or tenants if more than one) and a guarantor (if necessary).

Receiving the security deposit

A security deposit of approximately six weeks' rent is essential to protect you in case of damage to the property or furniture, or if the tenant fails to pay rent. This is *as well as* a month's rent upfront payment. This is normal procedure but if you feel that asking for a security deposit *and* a month up front will prevent certain tenants from applying, you will have to use your discretion. Students or DSS tenants will not have that amount of security, so there is an element of risk. I must stress, though, that I would never recommend not getting a deposit.

You will need to issue a receipt to confirm that you have received the deposit and this should be banked in a special account solely for this purpose. This money is not to be spent because it should be returned, with interest, at the end of the tenancy. Usually, with a letting agent, the money is kept by the agent in a separate account and cannot be accessed by the landlord.

If, however, there are damages or missing items at the end of the tenancy, the deductions can be made and the remaining amount returned to the tenant.

Collecting the rent

This is the nice bit! There are various ways to receive the money and I prefer to let my agent handle it, but you could receive it:

- directly into your bank

- through the post

- by personal collection.

Try to make it as easy as possible for the tenant, so the type of tenant you have will dictate the method. Some will pay by direct debit, which is ideal, while some will send a cheque through the post. The least attractive option is for you to go to the property every week or month to collect the rent, especially if you are not local. However, I know several landlords who deal with DSS tenants and this is the only option.

Tenants on housing benefit

If your tenant is on housing benefit, the local council will pay most of the rent. Arrange for the benefit cheques to be paid directly to you by asking the tenant to sign a consent form. Most councils pay four weeks in arrears, so bear this in mind when doing your calculations.

Expenses

However tempting it may be to spend the first cheque that flutters into your account – *don't*! Remember doing the sums? By the time you have:

- paid the mortgage

- paid the insurance

- paid the service charges

- paid the agent (if you are using one)

- paid for the inventory

- set aside for tax

- set aside for unexpected expenses

you may have very little left. Of course this depends on many things, but, I can assure you, in one of my flats I only make about

£47 a month. Becoming a landlord is not a guaranteed way to 'get rich quick', because most of us are in it for the long term, due to the capital growth.

CHECKLIST

Checklist for finding a tenant

Plan your marketing around the type of property and the tenant you would like. ☐

Advertise the property in papers, internet, etc. ☐

Speak to local companies or universities. ☐

Print out details. ☐

Take telephone enquiries with prepared information. ☐

Exchange details with applicants. ☐

After eliminations, call back those you think may be suitable and arrange viewing. ☐

Prepare the property for viewings. ☐

Arrange for a friend to be on hand during viewings. ☐

During viewings, go through your terms. ☐

Choose the most suitable tenant. ☐

Check out references. ☐

Draw up the contract or Assured Shorthold Tenancy. ☐

Take the deposit and bank it. ☐

Hand over keys on agreed date. ☐

Collect rent. ☐

The Assured Shorthold Tenancy

Renting out your property without a proper, signed agreement between you and the tenant is madness, in my opinion. Some landlords try to cut corners but in the end it isn't worth it. I always let my properties to a tenant who has signed an Assured Shorthold Tenancy, which protects both me and the tenant. This is usually drawn up by my letting agent, but it is possible to do it yourself with a 'tenancy kit' that can be bought from stationery shops or legal publishers. An Assured Shorthold Tenancy (AST) is an agreement between the landlord and tenant as defined by the Housing Act of 1988 (this was amended in 1996). It binds both parties to certain duties and obligations. The main features of a tenancy agreement are:

- the rent – how much rent is to be paid and how often

- how long – an AST can be for any length of time. I would always suggest a tenancy of six months or maybe one year with a six-month-break clause, which enables you to give them notice to leave, if you so wish

- expenses – it details who is liable for the various expenses involved with running the property (i.e. who pays for the gardening)

- the tenant's obligations – this sets out clearly the rules of the tenancy, such as maintenance, not to sublet, informing the landlord of any problems and reporting damage

- the landlord's obligations – this clarifies the landlord's relationship with the tenant and the property during the tenancy regarding privacy, structural repairs, maintaining water, electricity and gas supplies, etc.

- both the tenant and the landlord must sign the AST with both signatures witnessed by an independent party.

See the Appendix on p. 173 for an example of an Assured Shorthold Tenancy Agreement (AST).

Letting your property through an agent

Why you need one

There are many successful landlords out there who have never used a letting agent. I'm not one of them. If you have plenty of time, then great, but my advice is always use an agent. They can help in so many ways and relieve the burden of finding a tenant, but, more importantly, they provide an interface between you and the tenant.

Make sure you only use an agent who is part of an approved professional organisation.

The best letting agents are usually part of one of the main professional bodies such as the Association of Residential Lettings Agents (ARLA) or the National Approved Letting Scheme (NALS), which has a government-based code of standards for letting agents (see Useful Addresses for contact details). These organisations will offer protection to both landlords and tenants from incompetent agents who often operate without even a minimum level of professional indemnity insurance.

Choosing the agent

I usually select three agents in the area of the rental property and invite them to view. I have found in the past that the closer the agent is geographically to the property, the better. The good news is that you are not obliged to place your property exclusively with one agent. You can have as many letting agents as you like! However, if you instruct more than one agent to let your property they must all be quoting the same rental. Take advice on what your rent should be because they know what is realistically achievable in the current market. If your instincts tell you that this agent is honest, reliable and trustworthy and will let your property to a good tenant, then you can instruct them to go ahead and they will reply in writing with the agreed rental fee as discussed.

Most agents quote rent per calendar month with the very expensive properties being quoted per week. Ask to see their lettings brochures and examples of other properties that they have on their books to give you a feel for their style of marketing and ask about their 'Terms and Conditions of Business'. You may find that their rates are negotiable. Rather like selling your home, you need to shop around for a good letting agent that you feel you can get on with.

CASE STUDY

I had a miserable time choosing agents when I first started out because I didn't trust my instincts. There was one girl who kept telling me that she'd let my flat when in fact I don't think she'd even shown it to anybody. Eventually, after seeing several agents I came across a small agency run by three people I felt I could trust and who were very honest with me. I liked that and we are still doing business together.

CHECKLIST

Checklist for finding an agent

Choose an agent who is part of ARLA or NALS. ☐

Get three agents to view and quote on possible rental. ☐

Ask to see their brochures and Terms and Conditions. ☐

Choose an agency close to the property. ☐

Instruct one or all three agents. ☐

Agree the rent. ☐

Agree terms. ☐

What they cost

Most letting agents provide a variety of services so it really depends on your particular needs and how much hassle you are prepared to take. For example, if you are going to be living abroad you will need a full management service in order to deal with the day-to-day running of the property, like finding a plumber if there is a crisis.

If you are living around the corner from the property you may only want the basic letting service.

> Remember, some corporate tenants from the big international companies will not consider renting a property unless it is professionally managed.

So here, then, is a list of letting services that *most* agencies will provide and what they cost. However, these percentages can vary slightly from agent to agent and are also negotiable. If it says 10 per cent, they may accept 9 per cent. No harm in asking!

Basic letting service: 10%
This is of the total rent payable, payable in advance of the tenancy.

Letting and rent collection service: 12.5%
Although some agents include collecting the money by direct debit as part of their basic 10 per cent. If you are being charged 12.5 per cent this is usually payable at the same time as the rent is received (i.e. monthly).

Letting and management service: 15%
This varies, but usually you pay 10 per cent of the total rent in advance and 5 per cent at the same time as the rent is received.

Other costs

The tenancy agreement: £150
This is shared between the landlord and the tenant and is for drawing up the standard Assured Shorthold Tenancy Agreement. If the tenant renews his contract you will usually pay half that fee and split it with the tenant. This is in addition to the commission.

The inventory: variable
The cost for this will vary depending on the size of the property and whether it is furnished or not. It will include the check-in and check-out report. You should discuss this fee with your agent and the tenancy agreement should provide for the check-in to be paid for by the landlord and the check-out by the tenant.

Advertising: nil

The good news is that the advertising, marketing and photographing of your rental property is usually covered by the commission, but ask, as this can vary from agent to agent.

VAT is added to all commissions, fees and charges.

What you can expect for your money

The level of service will vary enormously from agent to agent so it is wise to ascertain exactly what they will and won't do. For example, one agent refused to give me the name of a plumber because I was not paying for a management service, whereas another agent was unexpectedly helpful and went out to buy some light bulbs for the flat without me even asking.

A good residential letting agent should do all of the following:

- offer pre-letting advice on presentation

- find you a suitable tenant

- take up references

- prepare the tenancy agreement

- collect the rent

- submit statements of account

- inspect the property

- deal with maintenance problems – if managing the property

- close the tenancy.

The levels of service offered by agents are the basic letting service, which may or may not include rent collection, and the more comprehensive letting and management service.

Basic letting service

Here is why it is worth parting with that 10 per cent (or thereabouts). You are offered peace of mind and the knowledge that if it *does* go horribly wrong, you *will* be able to get the tenant out.

For the basic letting service, the agent will do the following:

- Agree the rent to be quoted.

- Market your property appropriately.

- Find a tenant.

- Obtain references. These usually include their employer to confirm the tenant's salary, bank, solicitor, previous landlord. Make sure you are happy with the references. Unless you trust your agent implicitly, ask to see copies. Don't forget the contract is between *you* and the tenant. The agent is just a go-between, so make sure you are happy and ask as many questions as you like.

- Obtain your approval of the tenant.

- Prepare the tenancy agreement and obtain your signature and the tenant's signature.

- Arrange for an inventory and a check-in report to be prepared at the beginning of the tenancy.

- Collect and hold the security deposit. (This is usually six weeks' rent.)

- Notify the utility services – gas, electricity, telephone, water – of the change of tenant at the beginning and end of the tenancy.

- Notify the local authority about the change of occupant for council tax purposes.

- For 10 per cent some agents will also make sure that the rent, whether it be monthly or quarterly, goes straight into your bank account. They will then submit statements of account.

Letting and rent collection service

Some agents do not include the collection of rent in the basic letting service and will charge 12.5 per cent to do so.

Letting and management service

For 15 per cent, the agent will do a great deal more. Basically they are managing the property and dealing directly with the tenant to ensure a smooth tenancy, and will deal with every problem as it occurs. The letting and management service is ideal for the landlord who lives too far away from the property to make it feasible to maintain or for the landlord who is too busy. So, as well as all the other services, they will do the following:

- Pay the ground rent, insurance premiums, service charges, etc. from the rent received.

- Inspect the property three or four times a year.

- Deal with routine queries and requests such as 'Please can I have another table'.

- Deal with minor works or emergencies such as 'The boiler doesn't work'.

- Deal with redecoration, renewal, repairs and replacements. This is the bit I really enjoy but if you are out of the country they will do it with your verbal authority.

- Lodge any insurance claim.

- Organise professional cleaning after the tenancy and any repairs that are noted in the check-out report. These are paid from the rent.

- Obtain estimates if major redecoration is necessary.

THE LANDLORD AND TENANT ACT 1987

Section 48 of this Act stipulates that the tenant should be provided with an address in England or Wales for the landlord, so that the tenant may serve notices upon the landlord. If you live outside the UK, you must provide an address in England or Wales. This can be your agent's address. (The Landlord and Tenant Act is only applicable to England and Wales because Scotland and Northern Ireland have totally different land-holding laws.)

The contract

Some tenants can be fairly demanding and start asking for discounts if they pay several months up front. This is up to you but I always think that six months' rent is worth a little consideration. There will be certain clauses added to the standard contract depending on the circumstances but this is where a good agent can advise you on whether to go ahead or not.

Even though the tenant may say he wants the flat for a year, they will often ask for a break clause after six months. This is to protect him should he change his mind about the flat or should his circumstances change and he needs to move. He will need to give you two months' notice to quit or face a penalty. This is to protect you so that you have time to find another tenant.

In the Assured Shorthold Tenancy, it states that after six months you can give the tenant notice, if there is a problem. Two months' notice to quit, in writing, will be required. This has to be a special form, so get your solicitor or agent to do it. Remember if the tenant refuses to move out you cannot throw him out without obtaining a court order.

The rest of the contract stipulates basic rules and regulations such as: the tenant must keep the premises clean and in good condition; the tenant mustn't destroy anything; the tenant must clean the windows; the tenant must repair damage; the tenant must leave the premises exactly as he finds them; the tenant mustn't make a noise; cannot have pets; cannot lop down trees; cannot sublet; must pay the rent on time, etc. It's all fairly straightforward, but if you want it thoroughly explained, your solicitor, or indeed your agent, will take you through it.

Once the contract has been agreed and signed by both parties, and the date to commence tenancy has been fixed, the tenant can move into your property.

> You will need to provide several sets of keys to the agent and I usually keep a set in case of emergency.

Managing the property

Could you do it yourself?

The management of your property and your relationship with the tenant is the key to a successful tenancy. If you choose to manage the property yourself, you need to decide first whether you have the time to run around fixing things or whether finding a plumber in the middle of the night will be possible.

If you work full time you may find it difficult to be able to keep an eye on the running of your rental, especially when you have *more* than one. You need to think about rent collection and dealing with any number of problems.

If your rental property is a fair distance from where you live, I would think twice about managing it. Long-distance management is not ideal, so if it is more than three hours' drive away, I would use an agent.

I manage my properties because they are relatively trouble-free, with professionals who tend to settle in and go quiet after about two or three weeks. If, as a landlord, you have checked all the appliances and left instructions for the tenant, you have done your job. I always make sure they feel welcome and deal with any problems swiftly and discreetly. The tenant should be inconvenienced as little as possible.

Be professional

This is strictly a business relationship so it is important to keep it that way. Be polite, friendly and helpful but do not step over that line into friendship, because that is when trouble could occur. If you become too friendly with a tenant (never socialise with them), what will you do if he gets behind with his payments? What about damages that are uncovered when he checks out? Will you be able to withhold your friend's deposit? I think it could get very messy, so keep it businesslike.

Manage the property yourself if:

- you have the time

- it is not too far away

- the tenants are reliable

- you have reliable workmen (plumbers etc.)

- you don't mind tenants calling you at home

- you want to save the commission

- you'd like to keep an eye on the property

- you like dealing with people

If the reverse of any of the above applies to you, I suggest you use a letting agent to manage your property and save yourself the hassle.

Whether you are considering managing your property yourself or using an agent, here are some more management issues you need to remember:

- Insurance of the building and your contents is entirely the responsibility of the landlord. Your insurance company must be informed if the property is to be let. Some insurance companies get a bit twitchy about letting, so settle this first.

- The landlord pays for ground rent, service charges and general maintenance.

- Council tax is paid by the landlord when the property is empty.

- The tenant pays for gas, electricity, telephone, water rates and council tax during the tenancy.

- You must inform your mortgage company or anyone lending on the property that you intend to let the property. Some will require additional clauses protecting their interests in the tenancy agreements.

- Check your agent's 'empty property' policy. If the property is unoccupied for a while between tenancies will the agent check it regularly and will they charge to do so?

- Tax – if you are abroad for more than six months of the year you will need to obtain tax exemption from the Inland Revenue, otherwise the agent will deduct 23 per cent of the rent.

- Find out how long after the rent is due it is likely to be in your account, so you can adjust your standing orders. A slow agent, combined with the banking system, can mean that you don't get your money for two weeks or more after the rent is paid.

The horrors of being a landlord

I suppose if I'm honest there have been times when I wanted to chuck it all in and invest my money elsewhere. I thrive on harmony and stability and hate confrontation, so you would think that being a landlord wouldn't suit me at all. And yet, there are areas that are immensely satisfying. My husband says I'm a better negotiator than most people he knows and I adore the creative side of things and where else can you get a 10 per cent return at the moment?

So it's swings and roundabouts I'm afraid. As I said in Chapter 1, you need to be fit and good with people, but you also need to be tenacious, patient, diplomatic and motivated. I've had my share of stroppy tenants but generally I have been spared the really bad ones.

The most difficult part of being a landlord is facing up to the void periods when the market goes a bit quiet. This is the kind of situation that sorts the men from the boys. You need to be stoic and prepared to lower the rent quite dramatically. At least your property will be competitively priced. The way I see it, I'd rather have my flats let at a lower rent than have a void period of two months. It works out the same in the end. Most letting agents will agree.

The market goes through cycles of boom and gloom, when prices and rents vary according to the state of the economy, so as long as you are offering a flat to rent that is at the higher end of your particular market, you stand a good chance of attracting and keeping good tenants.

Also, renting is now becoming more the norm in the UK with statistics rising to over 12 per cent of the UK property market and I'm convinced this is set to rise even further with the change in demographics due to the huge rise in 'singletons'. So I'm in it for the long term and suggest you hang in there too.

If you are managing your rental property yourself, you will need to have a list of phone numbers close to hand, in case of emergency. Once you have found a good team, try to stick with them. You will need:

- a plumber – who is Corgi registered (so that he can issue the Gas Safety Certificate)

- an electrician

- a handyman for doing odd jobs

- a decorator

- a gardener – maybe

- a window cleaner

- a cleaner

- you will also need the number of the inventory clerk, your letting agent, your tenant's work or mobile number and, if it's a flat in a large block, the porter's number.

Letting your property in Scotland

To let out a property you should use a tenancy agreement, which is called a Short Assured Tenancy Agreement. This should be used in conjunction with an AT5 form, and an inventory agreed between the tenant and landlord at commencement. To bring the tenancy agreement to an end the landlord must serve a Notice to Quit and an AT6 form.

The Short Assured Tenancy Agreement for a residential property sets out the duties and responsibilities of the landlord and tenant.

The property or any part of it can be furnished or unfurnished and the tenant or tenants must be an individual or individuals (i.e. not a company or partnership).

It gives special rights to the landlord to repossess the property and special rights to the tenant to apply to a rent assessment committee for a rent determination in certain circumstances. A Short Assured Tenancy must be for at least six months initially and, before the tenancy begins, the landlord must also give the tenant a signed notice (Form AT5) stating that the tenancy is a Short Assured Tenancy. An inventory should also be prepared of the furnishings or equipment included in the let.

It is recommended that the tenancy agreement is prepared in duplicate and both copies should be signed by all parties, with both the landlord and tenant retaining a copy.

The form AT5 must be served on a prospective tenant by the landlord before the tenancy begins because it informs the tenant that the tenancy is a Short Assured Tenancy in terms of the Housing (Scotland) Act 1988.

Scottish Association of Landlords

The Scottish Association of Landlords (see Useful Addresses) is recognised by the Scottish Executive as the official body representing private landlords in Scotland.

CHAPTER 7

What to do during the tenancy

Preparing for the tenant to move in

Keeping the tenant happy

The end of the tenancy

Preparing for the next tenant

Preparing for the tenant to move in

Before you hand over the keys to your new tenant, there are several things you need to do or check on:

- Check the rental agreement (Assured Shorthold Tenancy – AST) has been signed.

- Make sure the property is ready to move into and that any last-minute repairs have been done. It is important that the property is in tip-top condition as this will be reflected in the check-in report and also will hopefully inspire the tenant to look after it.

- Check that the deposit has been received by your agent or by you.

- Check that the first month's rent has been received.

- Check that you have enough sets of keys.

- Arrange for a full inventory to be taken and checked. Take photographs of contents if necessary.

The inventory

The inventory is to protect the landlord's property and contents, so that at the end of the tenancy it is possible to see if any items have gone missing or are damaged in any way.

- All items listed should be fully described.

- All electrical goods should quote the make, model and serial numbers.

- Any already damaged items should be noted.

- If your flat is unfurnished, you won't necessarily need an inventory clerk but it helps to note the state of the property in detail to prevent an argument at the end of the tenancy. This report should be signed by both tenant and landlord. .

- An estate agent can recommend an inventory clerk or you could find one in the Yellow Pages. They are usually freelance.

Doing the inventory yourself

If you decide not to employ a professional, it is possible to draw up an inventory yourself, but this can be very time-consuming. The best format is on a room-by-room basis with three columns – for the item, condition and quality. You will also need to state the condition of the paintwork and carpets, so for example:

Sitting Room

Walls	Good condition	Small scuff to left of door
Door	Slight wear and tear	Handle loose
Sofa	Badly worn	Stain on left arm
Carpet	Badly worn in front of sofa	

You will need to produce two copies of the document, which will need to be dated and signed by both you and the tenant. Make sure you go through the inventory with the tenant when he moves in to make sure that he is happy with your descriptions. I always use an independent company to prepare the inventory because it seems more professional and gives the tenant the impression that you care about your property and your possessions.

CASE STUDY

Sometimes, a tenant of mine has supplied a replacement for an item that was broken but the item was not of the same quality or didn't match (my crockery), so by having a comprehensive inventory I was able to note this and deduct a small amount from the deposit in order to buy a more suitable replacement.

Handing over the keys

Hopefully, you are now at the stage where you, or your agent, can hand over the keys. I don't usually get involved in this procedure but of course without an agent you would need to go to the property and take the tenant through various things before you can hand him the keys and wave goodbye.

For example, he will need to go through the inventory with you and check that he is happy with it, then sign it. Give him a copy. Then you will need to show him where the meters are, and the stopcock and the fuse box, and the dustbins and the key to the back gate, and the central heating controls and the intercom, etc.

You'll be amazed how long this takes. You may need to show him how all the appliances work but unless they are particularly complicated, I would just leave a complete set of instructions.

All the utility services will have been notified of the change of tenant, either by you or your agent, but it is now up to the tenant to notify the services that he is the new occupier and for you to read the meters. Make a note of meter readings on the inventory.

I usually provide a list of telephone numbers, in case of emergency, neatly typed out and kept in a plastic sleeve. These will include my numbers, the agents, a plumber, electrician, management company, cleaners, window cleaners, etc. Of course, if the tenant has a crisis, he should call me first but it is comforting to know that some tenants are perfectly capable of dealing with a problem themselves. If there is a leak it needs to be dealt with swiftly and he might not be able to locate me.

It is also a nice gesture to provide a list of other numbers, such as the local taxi service, the doctor's surgery, cinema, good restaurants and information about the neighbours (could be tricky!), the rubbish collection, garden maintenance, the bus service and that sort of thing. Any extra guidance is always appreciated, particularly if the tenant is new to the area.

CASE STUDY

George Proud had one tenant who was flying in from America to take possession of a flat he had never seen. The agent left the keys with a neighbour because it was going to be quite late. So George left a box of provisions for him, such as milk, bread, coffee, butter and cheese. A bit corny he thought, but it worked a treat. The tenant was as good as gold from that moment on.

CHECKLIST

Checklist for handing over the keys

Go through the inventory together and, once agreed, ask him to sign it. ☐

Show the tenant around the premises pointing out all the hidden mysteries such as the stopcock for turning off the water, central heating controls, the fuse box, the intercom, etc. ☐

Read all the meters and write down readings. ☐

Hand over a complete set of operating instructions for washing machine, microwave, drier, oven, hob, vacuum cleaner, etc. ☐

Demonstrate appliances if necessary (but this is time-consuming). ☐

checklist continues

Discuss who to call in an emergency. ☐

Show him list of telephone numbers. ☐

Discuss other essentials such as rubbish collection, smoke detectors, security locks and garden equipment (if any). ☐

Show him the extra list of useful numbers. ☐

Make sure he understands the rules of the tenancy regarding making holes in walls, maintenance, pets and cleaning, etc. Even though it is all clearly stated in the agreement, it will help to talk them through. ☐

Hand over one set of keys per tenant in the property. ☐

Privacy and the tenant's rights

I always keep a set of keys to each property in case of emergencies and because I need to gain access occasionally to fix things for the tenant. But it is important to remember the following:

- The law is on the side of the tenant and you must respect his privacy. They have a 'legal estate' in the property and a right to treat the premises as their own.

- Always give 48 hours' notice if you need to do an inspection.

- You may only enter the premises with the tenant's permission.

- You cannot change the locks if you are unhappy with the tenant (see page 147 on eviction).

- You must not harass the tenant.

- You should never release the keys to anyone else.

Keeping the tenant happy

I know I've said this before but most tenants are good, honest people and the landlord shouldn't have any trouble if everything has been properly prepared, agreed and signed. The level of 'after care' provided by the landlord will also dictate how smoothly the tenancy progresses.

For example, if there is a problem in the first few weeks, jump into action, solve the problem and your tenant will be happy. Leave it for too long and your tenant could become extremely grumpy.

The settling-in period can be quite busy but in my experience it should be over quite quickly. In the early days I used to respond to every whim but now it is more practical to assess each individual situation. For example, one tenant rang me to say she couldn't get the oven to work. I'd only just checked it a week before so I asked her if it was switched on at the mains. 'Oh', she said. 'The oven is on now.' No visit required for that one.

On another occasion she rang to say the bathroom light wasn't working. I gently suggested she might like to change the bulb.

However, another tenant rang to say he had no hot water and the heating had packed up, so I went straight over to the property to see the situation for myself. A plumber was called round who then took one look at the boiler and pronounced it unfixable. A new one was ordered and fitted.

Basically, you need to decide:

> Can I deal with this on the phone?
>
> or
>
> Do I need to go round there?

You will very quickly discover whether your tenant is a whiner or a winner.

Always leave another contact telephone number if you are going away on holiday (if you have no managing agent) in case of emergencies, and make sure that person knows what to do. (It might help.)

Maintenance and inspections

Every six months or so it is advisable to pay a visit to your property to meet the tenant again and check that he is all right, the property is being cared for and to discuss any problems. Arrange the visit at least 48 hours in advance and take a checklist. (This will help make sure you have checked everything.)

Make the visit in daylight hours, so you can see the outside of the building, the garden, the garage, the path, the gutters, etc.

Keep the mood polite and friendly so as not to antagonise the tenant. He must understand that you *always* do these checks and it isn't personal.

- Check for any interior damage. Look in every room.

- Check all kitchen appliances are in working order.

- Take note of the general order.

These checks are essential to stay on top of maintenance. Real damage can occur from a tiny problem, so regular maintenance helps. 'A little and often' is my motto. Bad condensation can result in rotting window-sills for example, so you may wish you'd spotted the blocked ventilation.

Take lots of notes and discuss who will do what after the visit. If there is any internal damage you should ask him to repair it in a follow-up letter. The landlord is usually responsible for the structure of the building.

Dealing with maintenance problems

Generally, after a six-week period of teething troubles while the tenant gets used to his new abode, things quieten down and you stop dreading it every time the phone rings. I have found that it pays in the end if you appear to want to pamper your tenant and are keen to sort out any problem as swiftly as possible.

After a few calls they start to feel guilty about calling you and sort the problem out themselves. If you appear diffident or slow to react to a request they will ring more regularly and at unsociable times too.

CASE STUDY

I went to visit one of my flats a few years ago and discovered the family tenants had installed two rabbits. Very nice rabbits I'm sure, but there were droppings all over my carpet and the place stank. I remarked on the presence of the pets and was told they were leaving shortly. (The rabbits, not the tenants.) I didn't buy that, so I wrote a letter saying that the pets were breaking the terms of the lease and that I would need to use the deposit to replace the carpets. They accepted, thank goodness, and the rabbits went to a good home.

The end of the tenancy

With the end of the tenancy approaching you'll need to prepare for a whirlwind of activity if you want to minimise the void period between this tenancy and the next. I find preparation and list-making essential to prevent you going mad. I once had three flats vacated within two weeks of each other and nearly went bonkers trying to do the turnaround in record time. However, this is usually my favourite time as I can start getting all creative again

– painting doors, mending cushions, ordering new lamps and buying fabric.

Start booking decorators or tradespeople as *soon* as you know the moving-out date because the good ones are always busy and need plenty of advance warning.

Once you have received notice, or have given notice, for the tenancy to be terminated you will need to:

- Talk to your agent (if you have one) or start planning the re-marketing of the property.

- Make a final inspection of the property, taking note of any repairs or upgrading that is necessary. Does it need redecorating?

- Any damages? Will it need professional cleaning?

- Contact decorators, plumbers, cleaners or whoever may be required, to book them for the day after the check-out report (see page 131).

- Plan your redecoration programme carefully if upgrading of the property is required.

- Order furniture or contents replacements because these sometimes take up to four weeks to deliver.

- Plan your advertisements and start placing them in strategic publications.

- Start interviewing tenants to avoid a void.

- Call the tenant to make sure he is leaving when he said he would.

Most tenants should allow you to conduct viewings within the last month of their tenancy but how co-operative they are depends on their relationship with you. If it has been cordial it should be fine and the flat will be presented tidily, but I heard about one landlord whose tenant played loud music during the viewing, accompanied by lots of belching, and whose sink was overflowing with dirty dishes. Not exactly conducive to attracting a tenant.

The check-out report

The check-out is also known as the end-of-tenancy inspection and is where you can assess the condition of the property and its contents, with regard to returning the deposit. Personally, I find this encounter with the tenant (he should be there to speed the process) quite embarrassing, so my letting agent does it for me with an inventory clerk, but, of course, there is a charge for this. The agent or you should go through the property carefully to check:

- all personal belongings have been removed

- all rubbish has been removed

- the property is being handed over in the same condition

- the keys have been handed back

- he has a forwarding address.

The inventory clerk will go through the inventory to check for:

- damage

- missing items

- condition of appliances (and whether they are all working)

- state of property

- marks on walls, carpets, beds, etc.

- wear and tear

- general state of cleanliness

- condition of garden (if there is one).

He will also take meter readings. This report will then be forwarded to you and, after making your deductions for any damage, you can instruct your agent to return the balance of the deposit. Hopefully, by then, you will have your next tenant lined up.

Conducting the check-out

If you are doing this yourself, it is not as complicated in practice as it sounds but it is important to be thorough and fair to the tenant in order to avoid a landlord/tenant dispute over the security deposit. Diplomacy is required too because if your property is badly in need of a clean, just state matter-of-factly 'needs professional cleaning' and let him see you write it down. Hopefully, he will agree. A girlfriend of mine is more likely to say 'Oh, yuk', which is unlikely to gain any sympathy.

So, with notepad and pen in hand, you will need to do the following:

- Check the inventory thoroughly (see above), noting the condition – working order – of all appliances.

- Check for damage.

- Note the state of decoration, and carpets and curtains.

- Check that all his belongings have been removed (if not he must either remove them or pay for the removal).

- Take meter readings.

- Receive the keys.

- Get a forwarding address. (This is very important.)

- Discuss damages if necessary.

The good thing about having your tenant there at the check-out is that everything can be discussed on the day. If there are items missing or quite visible damages you can negotiate the amount you would like to deduct. He can tell you about the property, which may enhance its potential in the future (such as, 'We really needed a bigger mirror in the bathroom' or 'The vacuum cleaner is useless'). You could even return his deposit there and then, releasing you from any further contact with him.

> Take your time over the inventory and don't allow yourself to be rushed. If he is rushing you, it may be so that you don't notice certain things (carpet stains etc.). Don't make quick decisions either. If something needs considering, take the time to do so.

CHECKLIST

Things to look out for at check-out

Vacuum cleaner attachments have a habit of disappearing. ☐

Loo roll holders are usually either broken or wobbly. ☐

Ice-cube trays and fridge bits tend to go missing. ☐

Lampshades sometimes have burnt areas turned to the wall. ☐

Always look in the oven. It could be quite alarming. ☐

Finally, make sure the tenant has notified the local council tax office that he is moving and told the telephone company to terminate his account at that address. (This is why a forwarding address is so important. If his bills come to the flat you need to know where to send them.) It is up to the landlord to inform the utility companies of the change of tenancy.

Returning the security deposit

The security deposit often becomes a contentious issue and can give landlords a bad name if we don't play fair. To be honest, we'd be doing each other a favour if we all played by the same rules, because otherwise you create animosity between tenant and landlord. If you don't return the deposit – or some of it – the tenant is aggrieved and goes into the next property with an attitude, or worse.

When using a letting agent, the security deposit – usually six weeks' rent – is held by the agent. If not using an agent, it is held by you. This money should not be used as income.

In the lease, or rental agreement, between you and your tenant it should state clearly the terms under which the deposit may be forfeited. For example, you can withhold a portion of the deposit for:

- repairs or replacements

- any unpaid rent

- if the keys have not been returned and you need to change the locks

- redecoration that does not come under normal wear and tear

- any expensive cleaning of upholstery that is deemed beyond normal wear and tear

- damage caused by smoking if smokers are precluded in your contract

- the cost of disposing of rubbish or personal items that have been left behind

- any unpaid bills during the tenancy.

CASE STUDY

One of my tenants announced that she was leaving her flat in six weeks' time and would not be paying any more rent as we were holding her *six-week deposit* and that would cover it. I was horrified because not only is this against her contractual agreement, but if there was any damage to the flat, I wouldn't have her deposit to pay for it. Luckily there was no damage so I kept her deposit to pay for the missing rent.

Some agents will mediate over how much deposit to return, while other agents will not get involved unless you have a full management service. In that case, it is up to you to negotiate directly with the tenant. This is where a fully detailed check-out report is invaluable. When carried out by a third party there can be no dispute over a stained rug or cracked hob. The only dispute will be over how much to charge.

My tip here is – cover yourself, *but don't be greedy*. You may not deduct:

- for normal wear and tear

- for redecorating if the property was left in its original state.

Wear and tear *versus* damage

This is another grey area. Wear and tear is the usual or normal state that a property would be in after being inhabited for that length of time. So, if your tenant has been there for two years, you would expect the carpet to be slightly worn on a main thoroughfare or the skirtings to be slightly marked. You would expect the curtains to be dusty or dirty and the headboard slightly soiled. This is normal wear and tear. You cannot expect everything to be in the same condition after that length of time. If it is only six months you adjust your consideration accordingly.

However, if there is a hole in the carpet or a gash in the wardrobe, this is damage. If the fridge door is hanging off or a mirror is cracked, this is damage. These things should be discussed with the tenant and a suitable amount agreed for deduction. If there is any dispute, you should get a written quote or produce a receipt.

CHECKLIST

After completing the inspection and making your deductions:

Give your tenant a written copy of the costs incurred. ☐

Itemise the amounts you are holding. ☐

Supply receipts if necessary. ☐

Explain there might be a delay if you are waiting for quotes. ☐

Return the balance of the deposit. ☐

Make sure you have kept enough to cover your costs and *never* return the deposit before an inspection. Always get a receipt from the tenant for the amount you've returned.

Minimising wear and tear

• Do not allow smoking.

• Do not accept tenants with children.

- Let to professionals and not students.

- Buy good quality fixtures and fittings.

- Only let to females who are usually more house-proud than boys! (Sorry chaps.)

Preparing for the next tenant

Once the tenant has moved out I get the cleaners and decorators in and generally have a blitz on the flat. If you have pre-booked everyone and are fairly organised, the turnaround shouldn't take too long. Make sure all repairs are carried out and you haven't forgotten any, and remind the cleaners to do the oven, cooker hood and fridge, as well as everything else. These are often overlooked.

CHECKLIST

Checklist for preparing the property

Curtains should go to the cleaners with rugs, if any. ☐

Clean the windows too because it makes everything sparkle. ☐

Check the light bulbs. ☐

Check that all appliances are working again (they may have been moved during redecorating) and that the instruction manuals are visible. ☐

Change the shower curtain (this is a pet hate of mine). ☐

Your welcome pack should be checked. ☐

If you haven't already got a tenant waiting to move in, hopefully it won't be too long!

CHAPTER 8

Dealing with problems

How to avoid a void period

The tricky tenant

Evicting a tenant

How to avoid a void period

Every week that your property is empty is costing you money. Not only are you losing the rent, but you are also having to pay the council tax, rates and heating bills in winter to stop the property getting damp.

I have been in many situations where I thought I would never see another tenant again, but in the early days I only had myself to blame. In one case, the rent was too high because I had an over-ambitious letting agent who marketed my property to a very narrow field. I learnt from these mistakes and now make sure that my rents are competitively priced and that my flats appeal to the broadest market in my category.

There are ways to minimise these voids and there are various strategies that I adopt in times of crisis. Go through the list below if you are finding it difficult to attract a tenant and try to implement any changes as quickly as possible.

The quickest and most effective way to get a tenant is to drop the rent, but only do this if everything else is just right.

Minimising the gaps between tenants

- Have you advertised it properly? Some ads take a while to appear so make sure they are placed well before the end of the previous tenancy. This will give you time to show new tenants around, as in the last month of a tenancy you are entitled to bring people to view the property. It is probably a good idea to remain on friendly terms with your existing tenant so that he keeps the place tidy for viewings.

- Have you chosen the right letting agent for your property? They must be with ARLA, located close to the property and used to dealing with properties such as yours. Ask when they will start advertising.

- Are you being too fussy? I used to be emphatic about 'no students' and 'only professionals', but this was very short-sighted because there are plenty of good tenants out there who may not be professionals. I was narrowing my field by excluding certain people. So now I have had some students – mature students – and I even have a group of religious fanatics in another flat.

- You could also consider taking pets, if the managing agents allow it, and smokers, if you aren't vehemently against it. By stating 'no pets and no smokers' you are cutting out potential tenants.

- Is the decor going to put people off? I know I've said this before, but keeping it all very neutral is the only way to appeal to the widest market. Even if the walls are cream but you have flowery curtains, this could be enough to turn people off. Have a good look at the property before the end of the tenancy and make a list of all the things that need changing, and start ordering immediately. Ring the decorators if necessary.

- Have you checked out the competition? Sometimes it is worth looking at other flats in your area that are asking for the same rent because you may be surprised at what is on offer. For example, you may find that they all have really modern, state-of-the-art kitchens with ceramic floors and yours still has an old-fashioned cooker. Oops! Time to change.

- Is your flat in a high demand area? The quickest way to minimise the vacant periods is only to buy where demand is high. A local letting agent could help you with this. However, chances are that the purchase price will also be higher, so you will have to make sure that you are getting the yield you need.

- Do you need to change the ad and readvertise? Perhaps the wording could be changed – drop 'no pets' and insert a special feature such as 'two minutes from station'.

- Is it furnished? If it isn't you might consider furnishing it if the market requires it. All of mine are furnished because most young people don't have much furniture and like the flexibility.

- Would you consider a tenant on benefit? A DSS tenant and dealing with the council may not fit with your type of property and most investors try to avoid them, but I know several landlords who deal with their local council and make a very high yield.

- Have you targeted the right market? This is a bit obvious but is your property/tenant the perfect fit? If not, re-evaluate.

- Could you be more flexible with terms? If the perfect tenant comes along but she cannot afford the six weeks' security deposit plus the first month, perhaps you could come to an arrangement without being compromised. Take advice from the agent but I have done this is in the past and had the most charming tenant who was eternally grateful.

- Does your property have the 'wow' factor? When things got sticky I put wide-screen TVs and DVDs in two of the flats, which is not strictly necessary, but during viewings the general reaction was 'Wow. Is that staying?'

- And finally… Should you reduce the rent? Make sure your property is in line with other rental properties in the area and is comparable style-wise and then drop the rent. This should make you very competitive and guarantee a tenant.

The tricky tenant

Occasionally you might have the sort of tenant who likes to make demands and who complains a great deal. This is when having an agent between you and the tenant is ideal, because you don't have to deal with the hassle. If you manage the property, as I do, it means employing all one's skills of diplomacy and tact, especially if you value this tenant and want him to stay.

Keep the procedure very businesslike and deal with it as swiftly as possible. When contact is made, I always make notes and ask lots of questions and apologise profusely if I think it is necessary. (Sorry seems to go a long way.) If your tenant is sitting in a freezing flat because the boiler has broken down, deal with it quickly. A tricky tenant, however, is likely to complain about the slightest thing, so you will need to assess the situation carefully.

CASE STUDY

I had one girl who was always ringing me up for one reason or another. Firstly, it was to complain about the lack of storage space, so I sweetly reminded her that she had viewed the flat twice and had mentioned it then, so she was fully aware of the problem.

Then she asked me to remove a chair, which I did, and discovered that she had the largest hi-fi speakers in the world, crammed into a corner of the sitting room. She was also a smoker, and my lease specifies no smokers, so I had to mention it. Either she left or I would have to retain part of her deposit for extra cleaning. She accepted this arrangement.

She would then call about the light bulbs blowing. This is unreasonable as the landlord is not expected to replace light bulbs during the tenancy. I then received complaints, via the agent, of noise coming from her flat, so I had to ask her to be more considerate at night. It went on and on.

Remember, when dealing with your tenant:

- Most of them are normal, reasonable people who just want somewhere to live.

- Always remain businesslike.

- Be apologetic and polite.

- Write down all the information you can get about the particular problem.

- Keep a note of all contact.

- Ask lots of questions.

- Assess the situation.

- Act on it if you feel it is necessary.

- Contact your tenant to arrange a visit.

- Do not antagonise the tenant otherwise he may call even more frequently.

- If the tenant calls at unsociable hours, ask why and agree when it is acceptable.

- Never ignore a complaint.

- Most tenants go quiet after a couple of weeks, so do not despair.

Breaking the rules

If the tenant does something that he is not supposed to, such as painting the walls purple, smoking or having a pet on the premises, he is, in effect, breaking the terms of the lease. You can deal with this in one of two ways:

1. Smack his wrists and tell him to:
(a) repaint the walls, (b) stop smoking,
(c) get rid of the Irish wolfhound
   or
2. Give him two months' notice to leave.

The latter, in my opinion, is rather harsh but it depends on the individual circumstances. I would rather hang on to my tenants and then rectify the damage at the end of the tenancy. Just have a word with him about the terms and conditions of the lease and see whether you can come to an arrangement.

The disappearing tenant

Tenants sometimes vanish, leaving their accommodation unoccupied for long periods or may disappear entirely, before the end of their tenancy.

This may be in breach of the tenancy agreement as it usually states that the property must not be left unoccupied in excess of two weeks without informing the landlord.

This puts you in a tricky position for several reasons:

• Insurers usually stipulate that they must be informed if the property is to be unoccupied for periods in excess of 14 days, and may increase the premium due to the increased risk.

- Unoccupied properties can become targets for vandals and create nuisance complaints from neighbours, possibly then involving the local authorities.

- Unoccupied properties are vulnerable to occupation by squatters.

An important point is, is the rent still being paid? Even so, the tenant still has his rights, even if the rent has not been paid, and there are very severe penalties for any landlord who can be shown to have illegally evicted a tenant.

Not only is illegal eviction a criminal offence, the landlord can find himself at the receiving end of a claim for damages. This could amount to several thousand pounds.

What do you do if the tenant has abandoned the property?

Whatever the circumstances, never be tempted to change the locks and remove tenants' possessions. If you have handled the tenancy application properly you should always have sufficient information to contact the tenant or a relative.

You need the agreement of the tenant that he has actually abandoned his tenancy rights, preferably in writing. You also need him to return the keys – this is important, as returning the keys is a clear indication of the tenant's intent.

If the tenant appears to have disappeared, but you have no written confirmation, the important questions are these:

- Is the rent still being paid?

- Has the tenant left the keys to the property?

- Can you contact the tenant or a relative?

- Do neighbours have any knowledge?

- Can you see through the windows if the tenant's possessions are still in the accommodation?

If the above points indicate that the tenant has left and the property is in an insecure state, or you suspect it could present a danger to the property or neighbours, then, and only then, may you have a case for entering the premises and possibly fitting a secure lock.

If this is the case you should:

- have a reliable independent witness willing to confirm the circumstances

- leave a notice on the door informing the tenant that the lock has been changed and to contact you at the address supplied to obtain a replacement key

- not encourage squatters – keep the notices discreet

- not deprive the tenant of his rights to access.

Being careful may enable you to relet the property quickly (bear in mind that seeking a possession order can be a lengthy process). If the tenant does appear to have abandoned the property but other evidence introduces doubt, or you cannot confirm this, you should obtain a court possession order before taking over the property or reletting.

Evicting a tenant

This is such a complicated process and so painful for everyone involved that it is best to seek professional advice. Remember the tenant has his rights, so do not attempt to throw him out yourself as that is a criminal offence. It has to go through the courts.

There are usually only two reasons for eviction:

- the tenant won't leave after the tenancy agreement has expired

- he is eight weeks behind with his rental payment.

These are known as mandatory grounds for possession.

It is recommended that you hand eviction notices to the tenant personally. Hopefully, he won't respond with a bunch of fives! Make sure the paperwork is really accurate, as some judges will refuse to grant a possession order if there are any mistakes.

> If you decide to pursue eviction without the help of a solicitor, the Court Service publishes a series of leaflets, which are available at County Courts or online at www.courtservice.gov.uk.

The procedure is very lengthy and could result in you losing up to six months' rent and bearing the cost of solicitors' fees, so one alternative is to offer to pay your tenant to leave. Seems barmy I know, but one landlord I knew said that he offered a tenant one month's rent and kept the whole thing as civilised as possible, because as soon as it gets heated they are unlikely to co-operate. One month's rent will at least cover the deposit for their next accommodation.

Eviction is a tricky business and, as my solicitor was quick to point out, the theory is excellent but in practice it is another story. If the landlord has an Assured Shorthold Tenancy Agreement, which most of us have, it means he can serve two months' notice to quit and then gain possession. This is only if the tenant has been there for more than six months. If the tenant refuses to budge, you get a court order served and have him formally evicted but this can take three months. If the tenant has broken the terms of the lease the letting agents could start this process, but then you have to prove that he has not kept the property and contents in good repair and condition or whatever. As soon as a tenant starts being tricky, you should seek legal advice.

CHAPTER 9

Beating the competition

Upgrading the property

Attracting the tenant

Upgrading the property

You may feel that the end of a tenancy is a good time to upgrade your property in order to stay in line with the competition. You are right. With supply outstripping demand even in the rental hot spots, your property has to be the most desirable in order to attract the right tenant. It could be desirable in several ways:

- the location

- the price

- the style.

If the location is good (presumably you've done your homework before investing) and the price is right (i.e. you're not charging too much for what it is), it could be down to style. I'm not suggesting that every rental property should be designed with up-to-the-minute style because in fact that dates very quickly.

But it does need to look fresh, neutral and appealing. After a while a property can look jaded, so it needs more than redecorating to make it rentable. It needs an upgrade. An upgrade can either be a subtle upgrade or a radical upgrade.

The subtle upgrade

For this I would suggest:

- a new sofa

- new lamps

- new mattress

- change cupboard fronts in kitchen

- new vinyl in bathroom

- change taps in bathroom

- change curtains to blinds

- better storage.

The radical upgrade

This is fairly major and, of course, depends on your target market, but for a young professional couple paying good rent I would consider all of the above plus the following:

- New bathroom, to include new suite, tiles, power shower, taps, mirror, ceramic floor with underfloor heating, halogen down-lighters. Keep the tiles plain.

- New kitchen to include new worktops, tiles, units, ceramic floor and hob. New cooker, fridge, washing machine.

- Smart new furniture.

- Wood flooring.

- Uplighters in sitting room.

- Installation of cable, Broadband and all the latest technology.

- Installation of plasma screen TV and DVD.

Obviously, this is expensive but it can all be set against your taxation. In an increasingly competitive market it can be an investment worth making. However, having spent all this money, don't be tempted to put your rent up. You may find you have merely brought your property up to the same level as others in the area.

Attracting the tenant

There are many ways to ensure that your property continues to attract the right tenant, especially if the market is going a bit quiet. You cannot necessarily rely on your agent at all times, so it may require you being a lot more proactive with the marketing. Make sure your agent is advertising it in as broad a way as possible and is not merely responding to enquiries. For example, is it on the internet? Is it in the local paper? You could make some smart laser copies of the details and personally visit some local companies and ask them to distribute them among their employees.

CASE STUDY

Kate Fischer visited pubs, theatres, gyms and colleges armed with glossy leaflets of her flat in North London. She only targeted places where she knew her ideal tenant would be. She agreed it was tiring but her tenacity paid off every time.

You need to be absolutely sure that:

- the property is in a desirable area
- the rent is the going rate for that area
- the upgrade is complete
- the furnishings are good quality
- you have identified the market
- the agent is advertising it.

You will need to watch the trends to see what is happening in the market. Ask your letting agent for information about any new hot spots and areas that are coming up, especially if you are thinking of buying again. Watch out for new developments and find out if your local university is going into property for its students. Talk to the council housing department.

If all else fails you could try:

- reducing the rent

- furnishing the property, if it is unfurnished

- widening your target market

- talking to another letting agent for an honest opinion and some advice

- changing your marketing strategy.

Alternatively, you could sell! This might seem a bit dramatic because the property market does go through cycles depending on the interest rates and the economy, so I wouldn't give in too quickly. You should treat your property as a long-term investment and try to weather the storm. Sadly, I had to admit defeat on one occasion and sell a rental investment because it wouldn't let. If you get the true market value, sell and buy something else.

CHAPTER 10

Investing in the holiday rental market

Buying a second home

Furnishing a holiday home

Making a return on your investment

Buying a second home

I remember as a single girl living in central London being desperately jealous of friends who would whizz off to their country retreat every weekend. Of course, I'd get invited occasionally and would fall in love with the smell of wet Labradors, newly harvested fields and bonfires. Now that I am entrenched in deepest Gloucestershire, I am surrounded by those weekenders who leave their glorious homes to head back to the Smoke.

One of them asked me what she could do with her cottage when she relocates to Edinburgh. 'Put it on the rental market' was my swift reply. A charming house like that in a pretty Cotswold village should do extremely well. She could either let it on a long-term basis or on a weekly basis as a holiday let.

If you buy a second home as an investment in the holiday rental market, the same principles apply as the residential rental market, i.e. make sure it is in the right location and will let easily. This is not as simple as it sounds as holiday homes have a different set of problems, but get it right and you could be on to a little gold mine.

Where to buy

The best locations for holiday homes are dictated by a number of things: the foreign visitor; the tourist attractions; rural pursuits; and the countryside itself. Therefore a property close to towns such as York, Stratford-upon-Avon, Ludlow, Chester, Edinburgh, Windsor and so on are bound to do well.

A cottage in rural areas such as the Yorkshire Moors, the Lake District, the Welsh mountains, the Scottish Highlands or Devon, Cornwall, Suffolk and the Cotswolds will be in demand from walkers and climbers.

CASE STUDY

An old college friend of my husband has bought a croft in Scotland on the coast near Mallaig with three rentable units for walkers. I cannot tell you what a great investment that was because the place is constantly booked all through the year and they are now expanding. Since the advent of the internet, places such as this have become much more accessible and they now get bookings from all over the world. If your property is close to some obvious attraction, having your own website will be a tremendous advantage, especially if you can get it linked to other sites.

What to buy

The biggest demand is for two-bedroom cottages, which can sleep four or five, in an idyllic country location, but there is also demand for everything from tiny crofts to baronial castles, just not as much. If you are thinking of investing in this market, there are specialist holiday rental companies which will advise you on what and where to buy and send information packs on what is required, right down to the teaspoons.

The commissions they charge are extremely high, ranging from 21 per cent to as much as 49 per cent, depending on the service they provide, but the rents being charged are also much higher to compensate for this.

As most holiday homes have a weekly turnover it is advisable to hand over the administration, marketing and financial aspect to one of these companies as they are experts in their field and take all the hassle out of it. It is possible to run the bookings, advertising and maintenance yourself if you are on site but it can be hugely stressful simply because of the rapid turnarounds.

Also don't think that a holiday cottage will only be occupied during the summer months. Some properties are particularly popular over the Christmas period, especially the slightly larger houses (sleeping eight to ten) with real log fires. Two families will often get together for Christmas in a typical rural retreat. The school holidays are also an exceptionally busy time.

Finding a second home

- Do your research.

- Two-bedroom cottages let the easiest.

- Buy in idyllic rural location or

- Buy near tourist hot spot or

- Buy near the coast.

- Talk to holiday cottage rental companies, and get their brochure and information pack.

- Property must be fully furnished.

Furnishing a holiday home

The difference between decorating a rental investment and a holiday home investment is that where a rental property must be very neutral to suit all tastes, a holiday home can feel a lot more like your own personal home and should have a very comfy, lived-in, child-friendly ambience.

According to the holiday rental companies, the very traditional, cosy cottages let the best. If you have an inglenook fireplace you will score very highly. A thatched roof also appeals, as does a country-style kitchen. Remember, these people want an idealistic vision of the country style for a maximum of two weeks. They're not investing a lifetime in your property.

If you want to make money out of a holiday home you will need repeat business, and the furnishings and decor are an important part of guaranteeing that. If families are happy and comfortable in your home they may well return year after year. They need to be warm, have space and be able to sleep well. There is nothing worse than an uncomfortable bed.

If you can provide facilities such as a swimming pool, table tennis, sauna, tennis court, etc., then obviously that would be a bonus but is not really necessary. The holiday cottage companies will send you lists of what you should provide, which will include extras such as a cot, a high chair, a stair gate, an extra foldaway bed, etc. and washing facilities with full instructions.

Furnishing a holiday home

- The style should be cosy and warm.

- Choose hard-wearing fabrics.

- Keep chintziness to a minimum but make it cosy, not sterile.

- Use warm colours in fabrics and upholstery.

- Choose a heavy-duty carpet.

- Leave pictures, vases and rugs around to create a home from home.

- Buy good quality mattresses as they last longer and ensure repeat business.

- Make sure the heating is efficient and plenty of hot water can be provided.

- Provide good, clean linen.

- Provide extra duvets, blankets and pillows.

- There should be plenty of comfy chairs and sofas.

- There must be a TV, DVD, video and stereo. (Some even provide a good selection of videos.)

- Bathrooms don't need to be up to the minute, but a white suite is preferable and a shower is a plus.

- The kitchen should be fully equipped with enough crockery for however many the house can sleep. (Everything will be on the rental company's list.) Good cutlery is a plus.

- The whole place must exude a pleasant, comfortable air that makes people feel relaxed. That is the idea of a holiday, after all.

- Washing machine and dryer should have instructions nearby.

- One of the bedrooms should have twin beds.

CASE STUDY

Rebecca Tyrell stayed with her family in a beautiful house on the edge of Dartmoor. They had paid for a week but after the first night they all agreed that the beds were horrible and none of them could sleep. They were also cold as the heating was not nearly efficient enough. They stuck it out but vowed they would never go back. Unfortunately, they didn't complain to the owners or to the rental company so nobody was any the wiser, so presumably other families have had similar experiences. If you left a note encouraging tenants to write down their comments or complaints, it might be helpful and useful for your future reference.

Your house will be graded by an inspector from one of the holiday companies (if you choose to go through them) and they are likely to offer advice on any changes they deem necessary. They want you to get the highest rent, so they get a higher commission! Obviously, the more your house has to offer in terms of style, comfort, location and facilities the higher the grading will be. A grand Georgian rectory with eight bedrooms is bound to be in a higher band than a two-bedroom cottage but it won't necessarily let as frequently.

The regulations regarding gas, fire and electrical safety are the same as for non-holiday lettings, so all furnishings must meet fire protection standards and upholstery fabrics must be fire retardant.

Making a return on your investment

It is possible to make a very good return by investing in the holiday rental market but it is not without its pitfalls. It can be affected by the economic climate just like everything else, particularly in times of recession when the first expense people cut back on is leisure.

However, the business has now turned into a multi-million-pound industry and there are people going into it full time. Some buy a house with lots of land, outbuildings and barns, with a view to turning it all into a huge holiday leisure complex with many units.

I stayed in one in Devon with my family that had 21 units of great charm and comfort with a fabulous pool and after a few rough calculations we reckoned they were making approximately £80,000 net profit annually. Serious stuff. With the owners living in the main house, it means they can manage and oversee the units themselves.

However, running holiday homes is a notoriously fickle business on which it is extremely difficult to base any financial calculations. It certainly isn't based on 52 weeks of the year (except in some prime locations). With clever seasonal marketing you might be able to base it on 32 weeks of the year, but this makes budgeting your borrowings extremely difficult and sometimes raising a loan can prove impossible unless you have a substantial deposit. Remember, rents are disproportionately high on holiday lets, compared to long lets on an Assured Shorthold Tenancy. So, for example, a nice cottage in the Cotswolds might rent for £1,000 per week at peak season. Assuming it is only let for 16 weeks that would be £16,000 minus your commission (which varies from company to company) of roughly £4,000, leaving £12,000 out of which you have to pay all maintenance, borrowings, cleaners, laundry, repairs and tax. This might not seem too bad if you can cover all costs and still make a profit.

The biggest return on your investment, however, will be the capital growth. You have a solid asset that will increase in value. Rather like the private rental sector, it is not the rental yield that will make you rich (unless you have a lot of units), but the bricks and mortar itself. The basic rules apply. Buy a holiday home or second home in the right location, for a good price, make it look the business and in time you will see a return on your investment.

It is not for the faint-hearted, and if you are thinking of going into holiday homes in a big way, it will need 100 per cent commitment in order to make the business work. I don't think it is possible to run an operation like this as a sideline.

INSURANCE AND RATES

It is advisable to include public liability cover in your insurance policy. This covers you if a member of the public suffers injury or damage as a result of you or anyone acting on your behalf failing to take reasonable care.

If you let your holiday home for more than 140 days a year, the rates change from ordinary domestic to the more expensive business rates. Keep this in mind when calculating the income from your investment.

CHAPTER 11

Extending your portfolio

How to finance your portfolio

How to build your portfolio

How to finance your portfolio

So, now that you know the ropes and have experience as a land-lord, what next? Do you want your portfolio to grow so that you can sit back and relax during your retirement, safe in the knowledge that you have a secure income and several capital assets that you could sell? If you do, do you know how to do it?

I didn't realise, in my early days as a landlord, just how simple it was to expand my portfolio. I only have a few properties at the moment, but I am currently looking at expansion because interest rates are so low. The trick is remortgaging.

What is remortgaging?

Remortgaging is about releasing the equity that is locked up in the property that you already own. This happens as property prices rise over time so, for example, you bought your property two years ago for £60,000 and get it revalued for £80,000. With a loan of £45,000 this means you could access some of the £35,000 equity to buy more property, as you could use it as a down payment (deposit) to raise another mortgage.

> Your property value   £60,000
> Borrowings   £45,000
> Revalued by lender at £80,000
>   = £35,000 equity

If your lender is prepared to lend you 80 per cent of that equity it means you have access to £28,000.

So in fact, if you wanted to, you could buy two more flats for £60,000 each with a £12,000 deposit on each.

Of course, your initial mortgage payment will increase when

you remortgage but the other properties you buy will generate more income and the rentals should more than cover all your outgoings.

So you:

- revalue the property

- release equity

- borrow more money

- buy more property

- rent them out

- rental covers costs.

Every so often I ask a lender to revalue my properties so that I can borrow against them. Eventually you may want to consider putting all your properties with the same lender so that they can take into account your entire portfolio and give you, hopefully, a more favourable deal.

How to build your portfolio

There are several ways to build your portfolio and one of the quickest is to develop a good business relationship with your estate agent so that he alerts you first about any potential rental property coming on to the market. You will need to be ready to act swiftly to beat the competition. You must keep an eye on property price cycles to avoid buying when prices are at their peak so reading the property press is essential.

Try to identify up-and-coming areas before the developers move in but if they have already started developing an area, buying off plan at an early stage could get you 15 per cent discounts.

Spreading the risks

As with any business there is an element of risk. I've already covered the subject of void periods so it is essential to keep an eye on market conditions. For example, after 11 September, the London rental market bottomed out, so I quickly relocated to Oxford where I was told demand was high. I kept the London flats for the long term, but needed to spread the risk by investing in another area.

Similarly, some landlords spread their risk by not having all one 'type' of property. I only go for one-bedroom flats in smart areas but it could be wise to buy other types of property, such as student accommodation, if your research shows that there is demand.

The bottom line is, will your rental income cover your mortgage? If the market changes, you need to be on the case in order to minimise the risk.

- Can you drop the rent if accommodation in your area is already doing so?

- Never borrow too much.

- Watch out for the competition in the area.

- Raise your prices in line with market trends in order to maximise your profit margin.

- Get a friendly agent to tip you off.

- Negotiate with developers.

- If your loan is fixed rate and interest rates are coming down, remortgage at a lower rate.

- Watch the price cycles.

- Be prepared to negotiate with the lender.

- Spread the risk.

- Buy in different towns.

- Buy differing 'types' of property.

- Consider various types of tenant.

Conclusion

No one ever said it would be easy but Buying to Let has proved fruitful and worthwhile for me. Becoming a landlord and investing in property is not only providing financial security for my future, and my children's future, but has also given me a whole new career. Who would have thought that an actress of the 1970s and 80s would now be advising a new generation on investing in property? Bizarre, I admit. But not so unlikely.

What we all have in common is a need for a roof over our heads and some of us have identified a way of making money by being a provider of said roof. The style of landlord has changed from the wicked Rachman character of yesteryear, banging down the door to extract the rent, to a gentler, more stylish approach. Or so I like to think.

We are nurturing an increasingly transient population, who need flexibility, in line with our European neighbours. Most of them *never* buy and only ever rent. We, the British, are renowned as a nation of homeowners but I feel this is subtly changing. First-time buyers are leaving it later and later to take the plunge, so the indigenous market is expanding. I no longer depend on foreign visitors because I am tailoring my portfolio to a British market.

If I had a crystal ball I could answer all those frequently asked questions. What will happen to the rental market? Will supply continue to outstrip demand? Where are the hot spots? Who makes those crop circles?

But I don't. So I can't. That's what makes it so exciting.

LAWPACK
ENGLAND & WALES
ASSURED SHORTHOLD TENANCY AGREEMENT

Notes for Guidance

Insert date of agreement.

Dated

The address of the property to be let. For shared properties, be sure to identify clearly the tenant's room or part of the property, e.g. by giving it a number.

The Property

(hereinafter called 'the Property')

The landlord should give here an address in England and Wales.

The Landlord

(hereinafter called 'the Landlord')

of

This is the landlord's address for service of notices until the Tenant is notified of a different address in England and Wales.

Insert full name(s), and address(es) (if relevant) of every tenant.	The Tenant (hereinafter called 'the Tenant')	of _____ Where the Tenant consists of more than one person, they will all have joint and several liability under this Agreement (this means that they will each be liable for all sums due under this Agreement, not just liable for a proportionate part).
Insert name and address of guarantor. Delete if none.	The Guarantor (hereinafter called 'the Guarantor')	of _____ beginning on _____ ('the fixed period')
Insert period of term in weeks/months and date tenancy begins. ** Delete as applicable depending on whether rent is to be paid monthly or weekly.*	The Term	The tenancy will then continue, still subject to the terms and conditions set out in this Agreement, from **month to month/week to week*** from the end of this fixed period unless or until the Tenant gives notice that he wishes to end the Agreement as set out in clause 4 overleaf, or the Landlord serves on the Tenant a notice under Section 21 of the Housing Act 1988, or a new form of Agreement is entered into, or this Agreement is ended by consent or a court order.
* Delete as applicable. NB if rent is paid weekly, a rent book must be provided to the tenant.	The Rent	£ _____ per calendar **month/week*** by way of standing order into the Landlord's bank, details of which have been provided to the Tenant*.

† If paid weekly, give the day in the week e.g. Monday.	The Payment Date	The first payment to be made on the signing of this Agreement. All subsequent payments to be made **monthly/weekly*** in advance on the _____ day of the month/ _____ of **each week*†**.
NB The deposit should not exceed two months' rent.	The Deposit	£ _____ The Deposit to be held as security by the Landlord for any loss or damage caused by the breach of any of the Tenant's obligations under this Agreement, or any sum repayable by the Landlord to the Local Authority in respect of Housing Benefit paid direct to the Landlord. See also clause 5 overleaf.
Delete this section if there is no inventory.	The Inventory	Being the list of the Landlord's possessions at the Property and details of condition which has been signed by the Landlord and the Tenant, a copy of which is annexed hereto.

Assured Shorthold Tenancy Agreement *continues*

This Agreement is intended to create an assured shorthold tenancy as defined in the Housing Act 1988, as amended by the Housing Act 1996, and the provisions for the recovery of possession by the Landlord in that Act apply accordingly. The Tenant understands that the Landlord will be entitled to recover possession of the Property at the end of the Term.

[Under this Agreement, the Tenant will have exclusive occupation of his designated room and will share with other occupiers of the Property the use and facilities of the Property (including such bathroom, toilet, kitchen and sitting room facilities as may be at the Property).]

Delete paragraph if whole property is being let.

1. The Tenant's obligations:

1.1 To pay the Rent at the times and in the manner aforesaid.

1.2 [To pay all charges in respect of any electric, gas, water, telephonic and televisual services used at or supplied to the Property and Council Tax or any similar property tax that might be charged in addition to or replacement of it during the Term.] [To make a proportionate contribution to the costs of all charges in respect of any electric, gas, water and telephone or televisual services used at or supplied to the Property and Council Tax or any similar property tax that might be charged in addition to or replacement of it during the Term.]

Delete sentence which does not apply

1.3 To keep the items on the Inventory and the interior of the Property in a good and clean state and condition and not damage or injure the Property or the items on the Inventory (fair wear and tear excepted).

1.10 To allow the Landlord or anyone with the Landlord's written permission to enter the Property at reasonable times of the day to inspect its condition and state of repair, carry out any necessary repairs and gas inspections, or during the last month of the Term, show the Property to prospective new tenants, provided the Landlord has given 24 hours' prior written notice (except in emergency).

1.11 To pay the Landlord's reasonable costs reasonably incurred as a result of any breaches by the Tenant of his obligations under this Agreement.

1.12 To pay interest at the rate of 4% above the Bank of England base rate from time to time prevailing on any rent or other money due from the Tenant which remains unpaid for more that 14 days, interest to be paid from the date the payment fell due until payment.

1.4 To yield up the Property and the items on the Inventory (if any) at the end of the Term in the same clean state and condition it/they was/were in at the beginning of the Term (but the Tenant will not be responsible for fair wear and tear caused during normal use of the Property, and the items on the Inventory or for any damage covered by and recoverable under the insurance policy effected by the Landlord under clause 2.2).

1.5 Not make any alteration or addition to the Property nor without the Landlord's prior written consent (consent not to be withheld unreasonably) do any redecoration or painting of the Property.

1.6 Not do anything on or at the Property which:

1.6.1 may be or become a nuisance or annoyance to any other occupiers of the Property or owners or occupiers of adjoining or nearby premises

1.6.2 is illegal or immoral

1.6.3 may in any way affect the validity of the insurance of the Property and the items listed on the Inventory or cause an increase in the premium payable by the Landlord.

1.7 Not without the Landlord's prior consent (consent not to be withheld unreasonably) allow or keep any pet or any kind of animal at the Property.

1.8 Not use or occupy the Property in any way whatsoever other than as a private residence.

1.9 Not to assign, sublet, charge or part with or share possession or occupation of the Property (but see clause 4.1 below).

1.13 To provide the Landlord with a forwarding address when the tenancy comes to an end and to remove all rubbish and all personal items (including the Tenant's own furniture and equipment) from the Property before leaving.

2. The Landlord's obligations:

2.1 The Landlord agrees that the Tenant may live in the Property without unreasonable interruption from the Landlord or any person rightfully claiming under or in trust for the Landlord.

2.2 To insure the Property and the items listed on the Inventory and use all reasonable efforts to arrange for any damage caused by an insured risk to be remedied as soon as possible and to provide a copy of the insurance policy to the Tenant.

2.3 To keep in repair:

2.3.1 the structure and exterior of the Property (including drains, gutters amd external pipes)

2.3.2 the installations at the Property for the supply of water, gas and electricity and for sanitation (including basins, sinks, baths and sanitary conveniences), and

2.3.3 the installations at the Property for space heating and heating water.

2.4 But the Landlord will not be required to:

2.4.1 carry out works for which the Tenant is responsible by virtue of his duty to use the Property in a tenant-like manner

2.4.2 reinstate the Property in the case of damage or destruction if the insurers refuse to pay out the insurance money due to anything the Tenant has done or failed to do

2.4.3 rebuild or reinstate the Property in the case of destruction or damage of the Property by a risk not covered by the policy of insurance effected by the Landlord.

3. Guarantor

If there is a Guarantor, he guarantees that the Tenant will keep to his obligations in this agreement. The Guarantor agrees to pay on demand to the Landlord any money lawfully due to the Landlord by the Tenant.

4. Ending this Agreement

4.1 The Tenant cannot normally end this Agreement before the end of the Term. However, after the first three months of the Term, if the Tenant can find a suitable alternative tenant, and provided this alternative tenant is acceptable to the Landlord (the Landlord's approval not to be unreasonably withheld) the Tenant may give notice to end the tenancy on a date at least one month from the date that such approval is given by the Landlord. On the expiry of such notice, provided that the Tenant pays to the Landlord the reasonable expenses reasonably incurred by the Landlord in granting the necessary approval and in granting any new tenancy to the alternative tenant, the tenancy shall end.

Delete according to rental period

4.2 If the Tenant stays on after the end of the fixed Term, his tenancy will continue but will run from [month to month] [week to week] (a periodic tenancy). This periodic tenancy can be ended by the Tenant giving at least one month's written notice to the Landlord, the notice to expire at the end of a rental period.

reasonable deductions properly made by the Landlord to cover any reasonable costs incurred or losses caused to him by any breaches of the obligations in this Agreement by the Tenant. No interest will be payable to the Tenant in respect of the Deposit money.

5.2 The Deposit shall be repayable to the Tenant as soon as reasonably practicable, however the Landlord shall not be bound to return the Deposit until he is satisfied that no money is repayable to the Local Authority if the Tenant has been in receipt of Housing Benefit, and until after he has had a reasonable opportunity to assess the reasonable cost of any repairs required as a result of any breaches of his obligations by the Tenant or other sums properly due to the Landlord under clause 5.1. However, the Landlord shall not, save in exceptional circumstances, retain the Deposit for more than one month after the end of the tenancy.

5.3 If at any time during the Term the Landlord is obliged to deduct from the Deposit to satisfy the reasonable costs occasioned by any breaches of the obligations of the Tenant, the Tenant shall make such additional payments as are necessary to restore the full amount of the Deposit.

6. Other provisions

6.1 The Landlord hereby notifies the Tenant under Section 48 of the Landlord & Tenant Act 1987 that any notices (including notices in proceedings) should be served upon the Landlord at the address stated with the name of the Landlord overleaf.

4.3 if at any time:

4.3.1 any part of the Rent is outstanding for 21 days after becoming due (whether formally demanded or not) and/or

4.3.2 there is any breach, non-observance or non-performance by the Tenant of any covenant or other term of this Agreement which has been notified in writing to the Tenant and the Tenant has failed within a reasonable period of time to remedy the breach and/or pay reasonable compensation to the Landlord for the breach and/or

4.3.3 any of the grounds set out as Grounds 2, 8 or Grounds 10-15 (inclusive) (which relate to breach of any obligation by a Tenant) contained in the Housing Act 1988 Schedule 2 apply

the Landlord may recover possession of the Property and this Agreement shall come to an end. The Landlord retains all his other rights in respect of the Tenant's obligations under this Agreement. Note that if anyone is living at the Property or if the tenancy is an assured or assured shorthold tenancy then the Landlord must obtain a court order for possession before re-entering the Property. This clause does not affect the Tenant's rights under the Protection from Eviction Act 1977.

5. The Deposit

5.1 The Deposit will be held by the Landlord and will be refunded to the Tenant at the end of the Term (however it ends) at the forwarding address provided to the Landlord but less any

6.2 For stamp duty purposes, the Landlord and the Tenant confirm that there is no previous agreement to which this Agreement gives efect.

6.3 The Landlord shall be entitled to have and retain keys for all the doors to the Property but shall not be entitled to use these to enter the Property without the consent of the Tenant (save in an emergency).

6.4 Any notices or other documents shall be deemed served on the Tenant during the tenancy by either being left at the Property or by being sent to the Tenant at the Property by first-class post. If notices or other documents are served on the Tenant by post they shall be deemed served on the day after posting.

6.5 Any person other than the Tenant who pays all or part of the rent due under this Agreement to the Landlord shall be deemed to have made such payment as agent for and on behalf of the Tenant which the Landlord shall be entitled to assume without enquiry.

6.6 Any personal items left behind at the end of the tenancy after the Tenant has vacated (which the Tenant has not removed in accordance with clause 1.13 of this Agreement) shall be considered abandoned if they have not been removed within 14 days of written notice to the Tenant from the Landlord or if the Landlord has been unable to trace the Tenamt by taking reasonable steps to do so. After this period the Landlord may remove or dispose of the items as he thinks fit. The Tenant shall be liable for the reasonable disposal costs which may be deducted from the proceeds of sale (if any), and the Tenant shall remain liable for any balance. Any net proceeds of sale will be dealt with in the same way as the Deposit as set out in clause 5.2 above.

6.7 In the event of damage to or destruction of the Property by any of the risks insured against by the Landlord the Tenant shall be relieved from payment of the Rent to the extent that the Tenant's use and enjoyment of the Property is thereby prevented and from performance of its obligations as to the state and condition of the Property to the extent of and so long as there prevails such damage or destruction (except to the extent that the insurance is prejudiced by any act or default of the Tenant).

6.8 Where the context so admits:

6.8.1 The 'Landlord' includes the persons from time to time entitled to receive the Rent.

6.8.2 The 'Tenant' includes any persons deriving title under the Tenant.

6.8.3 The 'Property' includes any part or parts of the Property and all of the Landlord's fixtures and fittings at or upon the Property.

6.8.4 All references to the singular shall include the plural and vice versa and any obligations or liabilities of more than one person shall be joint and several (this means that they will each be liable for all sums due under this Agreement, not just liable for a proportionate part) and an obligation on the part of a party shall include an obligation not to allow or permit the breach of that obligation.

6.8.5 All references to 'he', 'him' and 'his' shall be taken to include 'she' 'her' and 'hers'.

Additional provisions
(if any)

_Insert here any additional
terms you would like
incorporated into the
Agreement._

Landlord signs here   Landlord's signature _____

Witness (if any) signs here   Witness's signature _____

All tenants sign here   Tenant's signature(s) _____

                                                    _____

                                                    _____

Witness (if any) signs here   Witness's signature _____

Guarantor signs here (if any) Guarantor's signature _____

Witness signs here   Witness's signature _____

Glossary

Here are some terms you may come across in connection with Buying to Let.

Advance The mortgage loan (also capital sum, principal sum).

All-risks insurance Insurance that covers everything that is not specifically excluded in the policy.

APR Annual Percentage Rates: the standard way of working out the true interest rate; the APR has to be shown by banks and building societies alongside their quoted rates for each mortgage, to enable potential borrowers to compare equally what is being offered.

ARLA Association of Residential Letting Agents.

Assignment The transfer of ownership to another person including property, insurance policies or a lease.

Assured Shorthold Tenancy (AST) An agreement between the landlord and the tenant, as defined by the Housing Act of 1988.

Balance outstanding The amount of loan owed at any one time.

Bonus Additional amounts paid on a policy.

Bridging loan A loan, usually from a bank, at very high interest rates to enable you to buy a house when you have been unable to sell your own.

Buy to let Buying a property with the sole intention of letting it to a paying tenant.

Buy to let mortgage A special mortgage to enable you to do the above.

Capital Money you have invested, not borrowed.

Capital growth The difference between what you paid for the property and what it is worth now.

Capital-reducing mortgage Repayment mortgage.

Charges Register One of the three registers maintained by the Land Registry for a property. It records interests adverse to the owner.

Commission Fee you pay to a letting agent.

Completion date The day when the money is paid, the deeds are handed over, the keys are released and you can move into, or begin to seek a tenant for, your house.

Conditions of sale The terms in the contract as stipulated by a buyer or seller to which he will agree to buy/sell the house.

Contract The agreement to sell the property. Not binding until exchange of contracts.

Conveyance A written document transferring unregistered land from the seller to the buyer.

Conveyancing The legal process involved in transferring the ownership of land or property from one owner to another.

Covenant A promise in a deed to undertake (if covenant is positive) or not do (if restrictive covenant) specified things.

Creditor Someone such as the lender who is owed money.

Deposit Money you put down to raise a mortgage.

Differentials When extra interest is charged on larger loans; these are known as differentials.

Early redemption Paying off a loan before the end of the mortgage term.

Early redemption charge The sum charged by a lender in the event of a loan being paid off before the end of the mortgage term. This is sometimes known as a penalty payment.

Easement A legal term meaning the use of another person's land – for example, a pathway across your neighbour's property.

Endowment mortgage A loan on which only interest is paid throughout the term; linked to an endowment policy.

Endowment policy An investment which can be linked to a mortgage loan to pay off the capital at the end of the term (or on death, if sooner).

Exchange of contracts When the agreement to buy or sell your house becomes legally binding.

Freehold The property and the land on which it sits will belong to you or your dependants indefinitely.

Gazumping The vendor accepts a higher offer even though he has already accepted yours.

Gross yield The annual rental income given as a percentage of the purchase price.

Guarantor Someone liable for all debts left by the tenant.

Indemnity covenant This is a clause in the contract in which the buyer agrees to take on any responsibility or legal obligations that the seller may have had.

Index map search A search to find out if ownership of a property is registered at the Land Registry.

Interest only mortgage You pay only the interest of the amount borrowed.

Inventory A prepared document listing all fixtures, fittings, contents and their condition in the property prior to the tenant moving in.

Joint tenants or tenants in common When two or more people co-own a property, if one were to die, his or her share would automatically pass to the other.

Land Certificate A certificate issued by the Land Registry to confirm the ownership of a house.

Land Registry The government department responsible for maintaining and amending the registration of all properties that have registered titles in England and Wales.

Leasehold The ownership of a property for a fixed number of years, granted by the freeholder.

Lessee A person who takes a lease (i.e. the tenant).

Lessor A person who grants a lease (i.e. the landlord).

Local search certificate An application made to the local authority for a certificate providing certain information about a property and the surrounding area.

Low-start mortgage A loan for which premiums start low and increase by a certain percentage each year until the full level premium is reached.

Mortgage A loan for which your house is the security or collateral. It gives to your lender the right to sell the property if the mortgage payments are not made.

Mortgage deed The document stating the conditions of your loan.

Mortgagee The lender.

Mortgage protection policy insurance (MPPI) An extra form of life insurance taken out by the borrower in case of death or illness.

Mortgagor The borrower.

National House Building Council (NHBC) This body provides a warranty to protect the buyer of new properties.

Office copy (entries) A copy of your Land Registry documents. The term also applies to other official copies – such as probates or letters of administration.

Preliminary enquiries The questions asked about a property before exchange of contracts.

Premium A monthly or one-off payment for an insurance policy.

Principal The amount of money that has been borrowed and on which interest is calculated.

Proprietorship Register Part of the Land Certificate, which records the names of the owners and any restrictions on their right to sell.

Redemption Paying off the loan at the end of the term.

Registered land Land that is registered at the Land Registry.

Remortgage Either you want to change lender to get a better rate or you wish to raise some extra money against the increased value of your property.

Repayment mortgage Loan on which the capital as well as interest is paid back throughout the period of the loan.

Repossession The lender takes possession of the property because the mortgage has not been paid.

Requisitions on title These are questions asked about the seller's ownership of the land and any matters raised before completion.

Retention A mortgage company will withhold part of your loan if you are carrying out extensive renovations or building a brand new house. They sometimes pay in instalments, depending on how well the work is progressing.

Service charge Extra charge to pay for the maintenance of the building in which you have a lease.

Stakeholder Someone who will hold the deposit as an intermediary between the buyer and seller. This is usually your solicitor.

'Subject to contract' These words should appear in every letter to the seller or his solicitor before contracts are exchanged. This is to protect the buyer in case it all goes wrong.

Surrender value The amount of money a policyholder receives if a life insurance policy is terminated before the expiry date (other than on death).

Term of mortgage The number of years at the end of which the loan is to be repaid.

Title The right to ownership of property.

Title deeds The documents conferring the ownership of land or property.

Top-up mortgage Additional mortgage from another lender when the first lender does not provide enough finance to purchase a house.

Transfer The Land Registry document transferring the ownership of the property from the seller to the buyer.

Unit-linked policy A life insurance policy under which the premiums buy units in an investment fund.

Vendor The seller.

Warranty A guarantee to accept responsibility for necessary repairs over a specified period such as provided by the NHBC.

Yield See **Gross yield**.

Useful addresses

Architects' Registration Council of the United Kingdom
73 Hallam Street,
London W1N 5LQ
Tel: 020 7580 5861   Fax: 020 7436 5269

The Architectural Association
34–36 Bedford Square,
London WC1B 3ES
Tel: 020 7887 4000   Fax: 020 7414 0782
Email: arch-assoc@arch-assoc.org.uk
Website: www.arch-assoc.org.uk

The Architecture and Surveying Institute (ASI)
St Mary House,
15A St Mary Street,
Chippenham,
Wiltshire SN15 3WD
Tel: 01249 444505   Fax: 01249 443602
Email: mail@asi.org.uk
Website: www.asi.org.uk

The Association of British Insurers
51–55 Gresham Street,
London EC2V 7HQ
Tel: 020 7600 3333   Fax: 020 7696 8999
Email: info@abi.org.uk
Website: www.abi.org.uk

The Association of Building Engineers (ABE)
Lutyens House,
Billing Brook Road,
Weston Favell,
Northamptonshire NN3 8NW
Tel: 01604 404121   Fax: 01604 784220
Email: buildengrs@aol.com

The Association of Plumbing and Heating Contractors (APHC)
14 Ensign House,
Ensign Business Centre,
Westwood Way,
Coventry CV4 8JA
Tel: 02476 470626   Fax: 02476 470942
Email: aphuk@aol.com
Website: www.licensedplumber.co.uk

Association of Relocation Agents
PO Box 189,
Diss,
Norfolk IP22 1PE
Tel: 08700 737475   Fax: 01359 251508
Email: info@relocationagents.com
Website: www.relocationagents.com

Association of Residential Letting Agents
ARLA Administration,
Maple House,
53–55 Woodside Road,
Amersham,
Bucks HP6 6AA
Tel: 01494 431680
Website: www.arla.co.uk

The British Association of Removers (BAR)
3 Churchill Court,
58 Station Road,
North Harrow,
Middlesex HA2 7SA
Tel: 020 8861 3331   Fax: 020 8861 3332
Email: info@bar.co.uk
Website: www.barmovers.com

The British Insurance Brokers' Association (BIBA)
BIBA House,
14 Bevis Marks,
London EC3A 7NT
Tel: 020 7623 9043   Fax: 020 7626 9676
Email: enquiries@biba.org.uk
Website: www.biba.org.uk

The British Wood Preserving and Damp-proofing Association
6 The Office Village,
4 Romford Road,
London E15 4EA
Tel: 020 8519 2588   Fax: 020 8519 3444
Email: info@bwpda.co.uk
Website: www.bwpda.co.uk

Builders' Merchants Federation
15 Soho Square,
London W1V 5FB
Tel: 020 7439 1753

Building Employers' Confederation
66 Cardiff Road,
Glan Y Llyn,
Cardiff CF15 7PQ
Tel: 029 2081 0681

The Building Societies Association (BSA)
3 Savile Row,
London W1Z 1AF
Tel: 020 7437 0655   Fax: 020 7734 6416
Website: www.bsa.org.uk

Cadw (Welsh Heritage)
Cathays Park,
Cardiff CF10 3NQ
Tel: 02920 500 200

Chartered Institute of Building Services Engineers
Delta House,
22 Balham High Road,
London SW12 9BS
Tel: 020 8675 5211

The Construction Federation
Construction House,
56–64 Leonard Street,
London EC2A 4JX
Tel: 020 7608 5000   Fax: 020 7608 5001
Email: enquiries@theCC.org.uk
Website: www.theCC.org.uk

Consumers' Association
2 Marylebone Road,
London NW1 4DF
Tel: 020 7830 6000

Corgi (The Council for Registered Gas Installers)
4 Elmwood,
Chineham Business Park,
Crockford Lane,
Basingstoke,
Hampshire RG24 8WG
Tel: 01256 372200
Website: www.corgi-gas.co.uk

**The Corporation of Insurance, Financial and Mortgage
Advisers (CIFMA)**
174 High Street,
Guildford,
Surrey GU1 3HW
Tel: 01483 539121   Fax: 01483 301847

Council for Licensed Conveyancers (CLC)
16 Glebe Road,
Chelmsford,
Essex CM1 1QG
Tel: 01245 349599 Fax: 01245 341300
Email: conveyancer@conveyancer.org.uk
Website: www.conveyancer.org.uk

The Council of Mortgage Lenders
3 Savile Row,
London W1X 1AF
Tel: 020 7440 2255   Fax: 020 7434 3791
Website: www.cml.org.uk

Department of the Environment, Transport and the Regions
Eland House,
Bressenden Place,
London SW1 5DU
Tel: 020 7890 3000
Website: www.detr.gov.uk

The Electrical Contractors' Association
ESCA House,
34 Palace Court,
Bayswater,
London W2 4HY
Tel: 020 7313 4800

The Electrical Contractors' Association of Scotland
Bush House,
Bush Estate,
Midlothain EH26 0SB
Tel: 0131 445 5577   Fax: 0131 445 5548
Email: ecas@fol.co.uk
Website: www.select.org.uk

English Heritage
23 Savile Row,
London, W1S 2ET
Tel: 020 7973 3000
Website: www.english-heritage.org.uk

Federation of Cable Services
Keswick House,
207 Anerley Road,
London SE20 8ER
Tel: 020 8778 5656   Fax: 020 8778 8402
Email: fcs@fcs.org.uk
Website: www.fcs.org.uk

The Federation of Master Builders
Gordon Fisher House,
14–15 Great James Street,
London WC1N 3DP
Tel: 020 7242 7583 Fax: 020 7242 0505
Website: www.fmb.org.uk

Fire Protection Association
Melrose Avenue,
Boreham Wood,
Herts WD6 2BJ
Tel: 020 8236 9700

The Georgian Group
6 Fitzroy Square,
London W1T 5DX
Tel: 020 7529 8920

Glass and Glazing Federation
44–48 Borough High Street,
London SE1 1XB
Tel: 020 7403 7177   Fax: 020 7357 7458

The Guarantee Protection Trust
27 London Road,
High Wycombe,
Buckinghamshire HP11 1BW
Tel: 01494 447049   Fax: 01494 465194
Email shirley@gptprotection.co.uk
Website: www.gptprotection.co.uk

Guild of Master Craftsmen
Prest House,
Exelby,
Bedale,
North Yorks DL8 2HB
Tel: 01677 427183

The Heating and Ventilating Contractors' Association (HVCA)
ESCA House,
34 Palace Court,
London W2 4JG
Tel: 020 7313 4900   Fax: 020 7727 9268
Email: contact@hvca.org.uk
Website: www.hvca.org.uk

Historic Scotland
133 Longmore House,
Salisbury Place,
Edinburgh EH9 1SH
Tel: 0131 668 8600

Home Buyer Legal Protection Ltd
8 Broad Street,
Wokingham,
Berkshire RG40 1AB
Tel: 0118 989 0914

The Housing Corporation
149 Tottenham Court Road,
London W1P 0BN
Tel: 020 7393 2000   Fax: 020 7393 2111
Website: www.housingcorp.gov.uk

The Independent Schools Information Service (ISIS)
Grosvenor Gardens House,
35–37 Grosvenor Gardens,
London SW1W 0BS
Tel: 020 7798 1500   Fax: 020 7798 1501
Email: national@isis.org.uk
Website: www.isis.org.uk

Institute of Electrical Engineers
Savoy Place,
London WC2R 0BL
Tel: 020 7240 1871

The Institute of Plumbing
64 Station Lane,
Hornchurch,
Essex RM12 6NB
Tel: 01708 472791

The Lands Tribunal for Scotland
1 Grosvenor Crescent,
Edinburgh EH12 5ER
Tel: 0131 225 7996   Fax: 0131 226 4812

The Law Commission
Conquest House,
37–38 John Street,
Theobalds Road,
London WC1N 2BQ
Tel: 020 7453 1220   Fax: 020 7453 1297
Email: chief.executive@lawcommission.gsi.gov.uk
Website: www.lawcom.gov.uk

Law Pack Publishing Ltd
76–89 Alscot Road,
London SE1 3AW
Tel: 020 7394 4040
Website: www.lawpack.co.uk

The Law Society
113 Chancery Lane,
London WC2A 1PL
Tel: 020 7242 1222   Fax: 020 7831 0344
Website: www.lawsociety.org.uk

The Law Society (Scotland)
26 Drumsheugh Gardens,
Edinburgh EH3 7YR
Tel: 0131 226 7411   Helpline: 0131 476 8137
Fax: 0131 225 2934
Email: lawscot@lawscot.org.uk
Website: www.lawscot.org.uk

Legal Services Ombudsman
22 Oxford Court,
Oxford Street,
Manchester M2 3WQ
Tel: 0161 236 9532   Fax: 0161 236 2651
Email: enquiries.olso@gtnet.gov.uk

Listed Property Owners Club
Tel: 01795 844939

The Location Company
1 Charlotte Street,
London W1T 1RB
Tel: 020 7637 7766
Website: www.thelocation.co.uk

National Approved Letting Scheme
PO Box 1843,
Warwick CV34 4ZA
Tel: 01926 496683
Website: www.nalscheme.co.uk

National Association of Citizens' Advice Bureaux
80–82 St John's Road,
Tunbridge Wells,
Kent TN 4 9PH
Tel: 01892 539275

The National Association of Estate Agents
Arbon House,
21 Jury Street,
Warwick CV34 4EH
Tel: 01926 496800   Fax: 01926 400953
Email: naea@dial.pipex.com
Website: www.naea.co.uk

National Federation of Roofing Contractors Limited
24 Weymouth Street,
London, W1N 4LX
Tel: 020 7436 0387 Fax: 020 7637 5215

The National Guild of Removers and Storers
22a High Street,
Chesham,
Buckinghamshire HP5 1EP
Tel: 01494 792279 Fax: 01494 792111
Website: www.ngrs.co.uk

The National House Building Council (NHBC)
NHBC,
Buildmark House,
Chiltern Avenue,
Amersham, Bucks HP6 5AP
Tel: 0845 845 6422
Website: www.nhbc.co.uk

National Home Improvement Advisory Service
NHIAS,
The Mount,
2 Woodstock Link,
Belfast BT6 8DD
Tel: 0800 0851 246
Website: www.nhias.org

The National Inspection Council for Electrical Installation Contracting (NICEIC)
Vintage House,
37 Albert Embankment,
London SE1 7UJ
Tel: 020 7564 2323 Fax: 020 7564 2370
Website: www.niceic.org.uk

National Register of Warranted Builders
Gordon Fisher House,
14–15 Great James Street,
London WC1N 3DP
Tel: 020 7404 4155

The New Home Marketing Board (NHMB)
56–64 Leonard Street,
London EX2A 4JX
Tel: 020 7608 5100   Fax: 020 7608 5101
Email: mca@wof.co.uk
Website: www.wof.co.uk

Northern Ireland Housing Executive
The Housing Centre,
2 Adelaide Street,
Belfast BT2 8PB
Tel: 01232 317000
Website: www.nihe.gov.uk

Office of Fair Trading
Field House,
15–25 Bream's Buildings,
London EC4A 1PR
Tel: 020 7211 8000

Office of the Ombudsman for Estate Agents
Beckett House,
4 Bridge Street,
Salisbury,
Wiltshire SP1 2LX
Tel: 01722 333306   Fax: 01722 332296
Email: post@oea.co.uk
Website: www.oea.co.uk

Office for the Supervision of Solicitors
Victoria Court,
8 Dormer Place,
Leamington Spa,
Warwickshire CV32 5AE
Tel: 01926 820082   Fax: 01926 431435
Website: ww.lawsociety.org.uk

Railtrack Property
26 Southwark Street,
London SE1 1TU
Tel: 020 7645 3000   Fax: 7645 3001

Registry of County Court Judgments
Registry Trust Ltd,
173–175 Cleveland Street,
London W1P 5PE
Tel: 020 7380 0133

The Royal Incorporation of Architects in Scotland (RIA Scotland)
15 Rutland Square,
Edinburgh EH1 2BE
Tel: 0131 229 7205
Clients' Advisory Service: 0131 229 7545   Fax: 0131 228 2188
Website: www.rias.org.uk

The Royal Institute of British Architects
66 Portland Place,
London W1B 1AD
Tel: 020 7580 5533
Website: www.architecture.com

The Royal Institute of Chartered Surveyors
Database Resource Centre,
Surveyor Court,
Westwood Way,
Coventry CV4 8JE
Tel: 020 7222 7000
Email: info@ricss.org
Website: www.rics.org

The Royal Institution of Chartered Surveyors in Scotland (RICS Scotland)
9 Manor Place,
Edinburgh EH3 7DN
Tel: 0131 225 7078   Fax: 0131 226 3599
Website: www.rics-scotland.org.uk

The Royal Society of Architects in Wales
Bute Building,
King Edward VII Avenue,
Cathays Park,
Cardiff CF10 3NB
Tel: 029 2087 4753   Fax: 029 2087 4926
Email: wrennm@cf.ac.uk

Royal Society of Ulster Architects
1 Mount Charles,
Belfast BT7 1NZ
Tel: 01232 323760

The Royal Town Planning Institute
26 Portland Place,
London W1N 4BE
Tel: 020 7636 9107   Fax: 020 7323 1582
Email: online@rtpi.org.uk
Website: www.rtpi.org.uk

Salvo
Tel: 01890 820333
Website: www.salvoweb.com
Organisation of architectural salvage companies.

Save
www.savebritainsheritage.org
A conservation charity with a list of homes in need of care and
attention.

Scottish Association of Landlords
47 Newhaven Main Street,
Edinburgh EH6 4NQ
Tel: 0131 551 6031
Website: www.scottishlandlords.com

Scottish and Northern Ireland Plumbing Employers' Federation
2 Walker Street,
Edinburgh EH3 7LB
Tel: 0131 2252255

The Scottish Building Employers Federation (SBEF)
Carron Grange,
Carrongrange Avenue,
Stenhousemuir FK5 3BQ
Tel: 01324 555550   Fax: 01324 555551
Email: info@scottishbuilding.co.uk

The Scottish Civic Trust
The Tobacco Merchant's House,
42 Miller Street,
Glasgow G1 1DT
Tel: 0141 221 1466   Fax: 0141 248 6952
Email: sct@scotnet.co.uk
Website: www.scotnet.co.uk/sct

The Small Landlords' Association
78 Tachbrook Street,
London SW1V 2NA
Tel: 020 7828 2445

The Society for Protection of Ancient Buildings
37 Spital Square,
London E1 6DY
Tel: 020 7377 1644   Fax: 020 7247 5296
Email: info@spab.org.uk
Website www.spab.org.uk

Solicitors Property Group
c/o Funnel and Perring,
192–193 Queens Road,
Hastings TN34 1RG
Tel: 01424 426287   Fax: 01424 434372

The Stationery Office Publications Centre
PO Box 29,
Norwich NR3 1GN
Tel: 08706 005522   Fax: 08706 005533
Email: book.enquiries@theso.co.uk
Website: www.ukstate.com

The Telecommunications Industry Association
Douglas House,
32–34 Simpson Road,
Fenny Stratford, Bletchley,
Milton Keynes,
Buckinghamshire MK1 1BA
Tel: 01908 645000   Fax: 01908 632263
Email: info@tia.org.uk

Timber and Brick Homes Information Council
Gable House,
40 High Street,
Rickmansworth,
Hertfordshire WD1 3ES
Tel: 01923 778136   Fax: 01923 720724

Twentieth Century Society
Tel: 020 7250 3857

Victorian Society
1 Priory Gardens,
Bedford Park,
London W4 1TT
Tel: 020 8994 1019
Website: www.victorian-society.org.uk

Useful websites

Property websites

www.08004homes.com
www.asertahome.com
www.easier.co.uk
www.estateagent.co.uk
www.findaproperty.com
www.fish4homes.co.uk
www.homepages.co.uk
www.homes-on-line.com
www.hometrack.co.uk
www.move.co.uk
www.properties-direct.com
www.propertyfinder.co.uk
www.propertymarket.co.uk
www.propertyworld.co.uk
www.rightmove.co.uk
www.ukpropertychannel.com
www.upmystreet.com
www.wotproperty.co.uk

Rental only websites

www.assuredproprentals.co.uk
www.citylets.co.uk
www.excel-property.co.uk
www.homelet.co.uk
www.letonthenet.com
www.lettingweb.com
www.net-lettings.co.uk
www.simplyrent.co.uk
www.spacetorent.com

Financial websites

www.financelink.co.uk
www.ftyourmoney.com
www.moneyextra.com
www.moneynet.co.uk
www.moneyquest.c.uk
www.thomweb.co.uk
www.yourmortgage.co.uk

Buy-to-let mortgage providers

www.bankofscotland.co.uk
www.bm-solutions.co.uk
www.bristol-west.co.uk
www.cheshirebs.co.uk
www.chlmortgages.co.uk
www.future-mortgages.co.uk
www.ipswich-bs.co.uk
www.kmc.co.uk
www.landg.com
www.mortgagesforbusiness.co.uk
www.northernrock.co.uk
www.paragon-mortgages.co.uk
www.royalbankscot.co.uk
www.scottishwidows.co.uk
www.standardlifebank.com
www.stroudandswindon.co.uk
www.woolwich.co.uk

Index